THE
GOSPEL
PEOPLE

The Gospel People of Latin America

Clayton L. ("Mike") Berg, Jr.
& Paul E. Pretiz

MARC, World Vision, International
Latin America Mission

© 1992. Latin America Mission

ISBN 0-912552-77-8

Published by **MARC, World Vision, International**
919 West Huntington Drive, Monrovia, CA 91016
and **Latin America Mission**
Post Office Box 52-7900, Miami, FL 33152-7900, USA

This book is affectionately dedicated to
W. DAYTON ROBERTS
a "wise old bird" from Latin America
esteemed colleague and mentor in the work
amigo/hermano/compañero en Cristo.

Contents

Foreword

I

Something is happening in Latin America that is so overpowering that all structures of the society as well as the value system of the various cultures of Latin America will all be changed by it. This "something" is an Evangelical revival.

Just fifty years ago Evangelicalism was a hardly noticed phenomenon in Central America and South America. Then, unexpectedly, there was a move on the part of the intellectual and economic elites of these Roman Catholic nations to open up the doors to Protestantism. The motivation was hardly spiritual. It was simply that they were cognizant of the fact that there was some kind of linkage between Protestantism and economic prosperity.

Some of them were well acquainted with Max Weber's classic study *The Protestant Ethic and the Spirit of Capitalism* and they knew Protestantism creates a state of consciousness that creates capitalism. Protestantism, according to Weber, creates the social/psychological character that leads to the amassing of wealth, the development of technology, and the efficient organizing of business. They felt that if Latin American nations were to escape from their socio-economic doldrums, they would need a new ideology and they believed that the new ideology might come from Protestantism.

It was not that they wanted to see Latin Americans become Protestants as much as they wanted their countries penetrated with the ethos of the Protestant work ethic and with the rational approach to life that is essential for national development.

This book clearly traces the evolution of the Protestant Church in Latin America with a special emphasis on that segment of Protestantism that has been labeled Evangelicalism. The book is important because it properly calls attention to the fact that Evangelicalism has grown from an almost insignificant presence 50 years ago to a sweeping revival movement today.

It should be noted that in Brazil, on any given Sunday, more Christians attend Evangelical worship than attend worship at Roman Catholic churches. In certain nations of Central America there is ample evidence that within the next few years, Evangelicalism will have swept into a position where it is the faith of the majority of the population. This book traces this incredible movement of the Spirit. It tries to point out the various intellectual, political, social, and religious movements and ideas that have contributed to this phenomenon.

This Evangelical revival has not been highlighted in the headlines of newspapers, nor has it made the cover of the prominent magazines. Instead, it is Liberation Theology that has caught the attention and the imagination of people in North America. Being a member of the informed intelligentsia seems to require identifying with the poor and oppressed with their political struggle for freedom and for economic well-being. In its most controversial forms, Liberation Theology has allowed for violence to be an acceptable tool for effecting the kind of social change that would enable oppressed nations to begin to approximate the ideal of the kingdom of God.

The insights of the Liberation Theologians have been discussed in depth in seminaries and religious colloquiums throughout the world. Those who have sought to demonstrate that they are in touch with what is going on in third-world countries, have read the Liberation Theologians and have communicated the idea that the thought of these scholars is the thought that has captivated the masses of Latin America. Nothing could be further from the truth.

While Liberation Theology has, in fact, made a great impact on the intellectual leap of Latin America, and while it is a commonly discussed ideology on the campuses of just about every university, it is not the religion of the common people. Those who work the fields and live in the barrios of Latin American cities have found their help and solace not in Liberation Theology, but in Evangelical Christianity. In the midst of everyday struggles of their arduous lives, they have found

in Jesus Christ a personal relationship that strengthens them to endure
what they must endure to survive. In the Scriptures, they have found
hope for themselves, even as they have lived in the midst of societal
systems that offer them very little in the way of optimistic prospects
for the future.

II

What fundamentalists and dispensationalists coming out of Bible
colleges in North America find difficult to face is that the evangelicalism
that is captivating the Latino consciousness tends to be predominately
of a Pentecostal cast. Charismatic Christianity seems omnipresent.
Those who come to the mission fields of Latin America with prior
judgments against "tongues" and "signs and wonders" are often
dismayed by what they find. Charismatic churches are growing like
wildfire, while traditional fundamentalism is experiencing a much
less spectacular growth pattern. What is even more significant is that
many who have gone to Latin America, convinced that the "gifts of
the Spirit" belong to another dispensation, have been shaken out of
that position and are coming to the acceptance that there is validity in
the activities, theologies, and worship of Charismatic Christianity.

Unfortunately, some missionaries have actually had to do a double
take. While in Latin America, they fully participate in Charismatic
Christianity, but when they are home with their more fundamentalistic
non-Charismatic support base, they have had to present themselves in
roles that are more in line with those traditions. This duplicity can not
go on forever. Sooner or later the truth must be known, Latin America
is not being taken over by Liberation Theology on the one hand nor by
Fundamentalistic Protestantism on the other. It is predominately a
charismatic movement that is sweeping millions into the church and
creating a whole new future for Latin American nations.

What is of special note to those of us in the social sciences, is that
this evangelical revival of Latin America has awesome political
ramifications. In many respects, it is being fostered by evangelicals in
North America who can aptly be described as representative of right
wing politics.

Those who have tried to examine the relationship of conservative
politics to Evangelical Christianity have warned that in Latin America

the linkage of Evangelicalism to the North American "New Right", might ultimately prove disastrous. A reaction, contends most social scientists, is bound to set in. Antagonism towards the political stance that is presently related to Evangelicalism in Central America and in South America may lead to painful opposition to what is now an on-going revival.

In this book there is a call for Evangelicalism with a social conscience. According to Mike Berg and Paul Pretiz, Evangelicalism must be socially concerned while at the same time avoiding alliances with political parties. A holistic Evangelicalism that addresses the problems of poverty without becoming identified with either the political left or the political right, is the best hope for Christianity within these nations. Through micro-economic development at the grass roots level, hope can be generated among the poor and a brand of Christianity that makes life, livable here on earth, can become viable.

There is no doubt that Christianity must sooner or later become involved in politics. But it is one thing for Christianity to identify with specific party interests and it is quite another for the Christian community to stand apart from the political process while speaking to it the things concerning the Scriptures. The Christian community must always stand in judgment of the political system, declaring the Word of God and helping those who are caught up in the political process to see the values of God's kingdom. It is the task of the church to point out the discrepancies between the existing social structures and the kind of society God wills for there to be here on earth.

This book points beyond the contemporary situation and gives us a glimpse of what the church must be and how Evangelicalism must speak to the people of Latin America if tomorrow is to be the glorious future that our Lord willed for it to be.

Latin America is important to the rest of the world, because it has a population explosion that can not be ignored. Its people by their sheer numbers will play more and more a role in global politics. Furthermore, the United States can not avoid what is happening in Latin America simply because people from these southern nations are invading our shores, populating our cities, and making their presence known in every sector of our society.

The Latinos are the fastest growing minority group in America and their future will largely determine the future of the rest of us.

The Latino culture which is impacting us is being molded by its religious faith. And the Latin America that is being created by that faith is a force that all people, Christian and otherwise, will have to reckon with in the years to come. That is what this book is about.

Tony Campolo
Eastern College
St. Davids, Pennsylvania

Introduction

Coming into Tegucigalpa's airport usually means skimming the tops of mountain ridges, slamming down on the runway and applying brakes quickly before the pavement ends at a cliff overlooking the small Honduran capital. There are no night operations at the Tocontín field.

The terminal building is simple and functional. Inside, cheap souvenir shops and the scars of numerous alterations give it the air of the back stage of a seedy theater.

We are in the mid-1980s, and olive green aircraft on the ramp suggest that the small, fragile country *is* the back stage to a larger drama. Who are all those passengers boarding the next flight out?

—Military advisors for the then CIA-sponsored "covert" war against the Nicaraguan Sandinistas?

—Executives of the fruit companies on the coast — powerful transnational enterprises that can steamroller a tiny banana republic into granting lucrative land concessions?

—Communists maneuvering to control the country's labor unions?

Just observing them, its hard to say. But you can be sure they are all players on the stage.

Hondurans themselves have become involved in the international geo-political drama. Graffiti on the terminal wall express their feelings:

"Poor Honduras — oppressed and occupied"
This is the voice of the Latin American who resists past and present colonialism. This is the angry hand that a dozen years earlier designed

an anti-American poster twisting the "x" of Nixon into a swastika.

"You s.o.b. communist: go back to Cuba"
Scrawled by a different hand, the second line is the expression of those eager for stability — those nervous about the guerrillas in the hills, or those of the far right who see a menace in every move to change the system. Of these people, the saying goes, "They will find communists even in their soup."
And one last line, below the other two, by yet another author:

"Christ is the answer!"
This may be a triumphal declaration by an evangelical Christian.

He reflects a movement which in the last 30 years has become a voting block for politicians to woo, a thorn in the side of the Roman Catholic hierarchy, and a new option for millions who see no final answer in either Communism or capitalism — only in Christ.

These are the *evangélicos* — those who follow the *evangelio*, the gospel. They can be called the "Gospel People". In Argentina and Mexico they are labeled *evangelistas*, or evangelists. In other places smilingly identified as the *panderetas* (the "tambourines"), or the *aleluyas*, because of what neighbors hear when they pass evangelical meeting places.

Only recently has the word *protestante* become somewhat common. It is often used by government officials with careless disregard for the distinctions between Presbyterians and Jehovah's Witnesses. Latin Americans prefer *evangélico*. The word sounds less abrasive than *protestante* ("All you do is protest?") and *evangélico* identifies the movement with an evangelical theological posture. It used to be said that in Latin America all *evangélicos* were evangelical. Although some have become less so, the name still sticks.

It is especially appropriate to call them the "Gospel People" in Latin America because of their message of salvation by faith alone — the gospel of grace and power — of Luther and the great reformers. This contrasts sharply with the traditionally complicated Roman Catholic practices.

Two Basic Questions

Two questions arise as we think of this new evangelical force in the countries south of the border.

First, *what makes the Gospel People grow?* A recent cartoon depicted a Moses-kind of person descending from the mount with tablets of stone. At the base was a group of disheartened, apparently Anglo clergy, anxious to hear some word of encouragement. "What do the tablets say?" they ask. His reply: "I dunno; it's in Spanish."

Some observers hint that God is especially favoring the Latin American church. Researcher David Barrett estimates that by AD 2000 the Spanish-speaking *mestizo* (Spanish-Indian) population will be the largest single Christian ethno-linguistic group in the world (His definition includes all forms of Christianity). The "Gospel People" are a large and fast-growing segment of this group.

We look at the graffiti in the Honduran airport and ponder over the third line. *How can Christ be the answer to the misery, the violence and the sin of this vast region?* This is our second question.

"Christ is the answer" can mean different things to different people. Some see Him providing only a hope for the future when He returns. Others, the individual conversion of millions of people as creating a new moral force which could change the whole Latin American scene. Still others see only the emergence of a whole new social system, more Christian in its concern for the common man.

To answer these two questions, we must look at the context in which the Gospel People live and witness. Latin America's religious context is nominally Roman Catholicism. But for the *evangélicos*, cooperation with the hierarchy of the Latin American Catholic Church is often inconceivable.

Poverty — the economic context — helps us understand why most *evangélicos* are drawn from the poorest classes, who find no hope for *mañana*.

While some *evangélicos* ("Gospel People") may now be less evangelical (less evangelistically fervent), some non-*evangélicos*, including many Roman Catholics, are becoming more evangelical. The lines between the groups are blurred. Strictly speaking, we should include more than the *evangélicos* in describing the rise of the Gospel People. However, the evangelical movement in Latin America will be this book's central focus, especially from the 1950's to the 1990's.

Generalizations abound in an overview like this! People knowledgeable about Latin America will find exceptions to our observations. We will refer, for example, to mainline denominations entering Latin America before the faith missions. We know of one country where this is not true. But this does not invalidate the general rule. This is a book about "the general rules."

In it, you will find descriptions rather than numerous statistics — anecdotes rather than excessive formal analyses. It is our hope that you will be moved by them, and by this exposure to Latin American *realidades* ("realities"). More than that, we pray you will develop a spiritual bond with our brothers and sisters of the Latin American evangelical church, the Gospel People.

We are deeply grateful for our Latin America Mission colleagues' prayers and encouragement in this endeavor. Great appreciation is expressed for the critical and invaluable work provided by editorial readers of the manuscript, all of whom are related to the LAM either as missionaries, board or general council members, or supporting Mission friends. They are: LAM President Paul Landrey, Paul Borthwick, Guillermo Cook, John Huffman, Eileen F. Moffett, Robert Reekie, Dayton Roberts, Nancy Campbell Schell, John Stam, and Marlene Medefind Van Brocklin.

The authors

Miami, Florida
San José, Costa Rica

Prologue

The casket wobbled and nearly slipped off the shoulders of the four brothers as they stumbled to the burial site. Women gasped and frantic hands reached out to steady their burden as it was lowered and slid into a niche. A mason sealed the opening with brick and mortar, the clinking of his trowel adding a final note. The pallbearers' aged father had finally come to rest.

Mario, the oldest of the brothers, was not drunk. A strong rough-hewn man, he sweated out his livelihood swinging his *machete* to cut the lawns of the rich. Although he owned a tiny house on the edge of the fast-growing city, it was at the bottom of the hill, often flooded by the adjacent stream. Until recently, his drinking habit had worked against keeping food on the family table.

Painfully aware of his shortcomings as a husband and father, Mario had begun attending a gospel service in Antonio's house down the street. There, one night, he interrupted the preacher by standing up in the middle of the sermon to declare: "If anyone needs to accept Christ, it's me!"

Antonio was fortunate. He had a steady job. An evangelical Christian, he had turned onehalf of his scrap-lumber house into a meeting place by crowding his children's beds into the tiny living area. The "chapel" was furnished with backless benches and illuminated by a single bare light dangling from the ceiling.

Despite the humble meeting place, Antonio's guitar music and simple messages touched the lives of his neighbors who dropped in. A church was born.

The gospel also touched Mario's family. His wife, who added to the family income as a maid, also accepted Christ. And his son, Francisco, did, too. Barely literate, he followed his father's footsteps as a gardener. But another son spent half of his years in a reformatory and one daughter became a teenage single mother.

But Ana María, another daughter, was a pretty teenager who committed her life to Christ in Antonio's house and stood firm in an environment where only God could keep her safe. She smilingly took charge of her younger siblings, taught in Sunday School, and was often first to speak when testimonies were called for.

"I want to serve God more than anything else," she told a missionary friend. But hopes failed when she had to drop out of school to become a maid. The job turned out to be a classic case of exploitation. At one crisis she called her spiritual mentor. The missionary had an idea.

"If you're quitting, here's your chance to go to Bible School," she suggested.

"But how could I possibly pay for that?"

"God has his ways. Look, if God wants you to quit, we can leave this afternoon and visit the school. We'll see if they accept you."

That afternoon they drove to the coast. The ocean, though only 85 miles away, opened up a new vista for Ana María. They watched the sun set as they crossed the bay on a rusty ferry. The next day they stopped to look at the school and a month later she checked in.

From out of the mire at the bottom of Latin America's society, God caused another flower to bloom.

The story does not end here. It concludes in the epilogue.

CHAPTER ONE

Bandits, slaves and earthquakes

The lazy Saturday afternoon quiet at Vicente Mendoza's isolated farm was broken by the sudden arrival of five armed men. Vicente jumped quickly from his hammock to defend his common-law wife, his family and visitors.

Unprepared to offer much resistance, Vicente was beaten severely and the women tied up. As the bandits began to sack the house, their only explanation was: "You are evangelicals; we are communists."

One climbed up on the thatched roof to set it on fire. But Vicente's wife pleaded so pitifully for mercy for the sake of the small children that he desisted.

Before the men left with the loot, they heeded the pleas of another woman. She was untied so she could attend to the traumatized children.

The raid left Vicente with only the pajamas he was wearing. Everything else was gone. "There's not even a match left in the house," he reported afterwards.

This is the north coast of Colombia, South America, land of novelist Gabriel García Marquez. He describes the area in terms of languid surrender to the oppressive heat and the passions that erupt in primitive violence.

The year was 1963, and the worst of Colombia's violence was over. The ten year civil war (1948-1958) had ended with its toll of 300,000 lives. The war had made banditry a way of life.

How much of the bandit attack was common criminality? How much was supply-gathering for the incipient guerrilla movements?

How much was religious persecution? No one knows. Said David Howard, missionary in the area at the time, "What the motives were, or who was behind it, if anyone, is not clear."

Another Side of the Story

That same area was ablaze at the time in wild-fire response to the gospel. Missionaries had perspired and persevered over soil that had only grudgingly yielded spiritual fruit. But now, entire villages were turning to Christ because of God's sovereign work. Centuries of events had shaped the way.

Life was cheap. The years of violence made it so. Poverty left people in despair. A medieval Catholicism left a legacy of too few priests and a closed Bible. But there was enough truth for many to realize there was something more.

The political positions people took were unbending. The poor were always the victims. A wealthy Colombian rancher in the area was asked, "Why not sell unused parcels of land to the landless poor?" He replied, "They're communists."

But, "Do you understand what we mean?" the questioner persisted. "Not *give* them land, but *sell* it to them over a long term at a fair price." "They're communists."

African slaves were disembarked at nearby Cartagena de las Indias centuries before. Their descendants became a racial mix that was more sunny, spontaneous and expressive. They were more willing to hear and more willing to communicate than the descendants of Spain who lived in the clouded and rainy mountain cities in other parts of the country.

Violence directed against evangelicals produced in them a character that stood firm despite opposition. A character willing to take risks in sharing the gospel.

Attacks on the Vicente Mendozas, together with racial blending, political struggle, economic hardship and the entrance of the gospel all converged to set the stage for God to intervene mightily.

A Gospel Tent in Zone 9

A huge blue and yellow tent is erected on the lawn of one of the spacious homes of Zone 9 in Guatemala City. Chic boutiques and residences of the wealthy hidden behind high walls in this part of town hardly seem the appropriate setting for a tent meeting. This is the middle-class "Church of Jesus Christ." Members are hard put to find parking spaces along the tree-lined avenues. No dirt underfoot — this is a well-paved permanent installation. Ushers uniformly dressed in neat beige suits lead people to their seats. Banks of flowers adorn

Colombian evangelicals view their ruined church during time of violence in the 1950's.

the platform. A sophisticated sound-mixer assures good listening.

"There are moments, when words fail
to say how I feel, Blessed Savior . . . "

The congregation sings the chorus reverently, accompanied by a uniformed musical group playing an electric piano, guitars and drums. Livelier choruses had been sung earlier in the service.

The service lasts two and one half hours, but with the attractive music and the dynamic preacher there is no sense that the time has dragged. The pastor, in a business suit, seems more like a corporation executive. In fact, he is a former business consultant. He raised up this congregation in only a year. Of course he had a TV ministry previously, so his name and face were well known. Although already successful as the founder of a church, he is pursuing seminary studies. This comes through in the Biblical content of his message.

As in northern Colombia, this phenomenon did not occur without historical antecedents.

A devastating earthquake in 1976 left much of Guatemala in ruins. The adobe walls of homes crumbled and heavy tiled roofs crushed sleeping occupants.

Help from U.S. Christians was quick and plentiful. Volunteers constructed wooden platforms with the pattern of the side of a house prepared on it. Lumber was cut quickly with power saws and laid on the platforms to fit the pattern. Framing was nailed to the boards, the whole thing was then lifted away — a prefab side of a simple house ready to be taken to the home site.

This kind of ready assistance demonstrated Christian love. It was not hard to follow up with the message. And new evangelical ministries flooded the country.

But there are darker sides to the picture. Indians, oppressed for centuries by the Spanish and *mestizos*, often allied themselves with guerrilla groups bent on revolution. If not identified with the guerrillas, they were at least caught in the cross-fire. As government forces attacked, thousands fled across the border to Mexico. The U.S. cut off military aid to Guatemala, given the atrocities and the bad human rights record of the government.

The Roman Catholic Church for many years took the side of the poor and the Indian. But this left many Guatemalans feeling betrayed by their church.

A military coup brought an evangelical general, Efraín Ríos Montt, to the presidency in Guatemala's "Green Palace." He conducted his version of Franklin D. Roosevelt's "Fireside Chats" every Sunday, begging the guerrillas to lay down their arms and businessmen to hold down their prices so that the poor could survive. But the rifts in society were already too deep. The fighting continued and Ríos Montt's record is not universally admired.

With the events of the previous years, one thing now became certain — there were other religious options.

"God is Love" is the message across the top of many a bus windshield. A street preacher with a bullhorn preaches a gospel message on Sunday afternoon just a block away from the President's palace and the Cathedral. Station TGN of CAM International and a Pentecostal radio station give testimony on the airwaves. Not through a freak circumstance, but as a result of a formal election, an evangelical candidate gets elected to the office of president.

One hundred years of Protestant witness is celebrated in 1982. Evangelical pastors and leaders meet, declaring that their goal is to see Guatemala 50% evangelical by 1990. To prove that such a goal was achieved is not easy. Indian villages with their evangelical chapels are remote. Storefront churches in the city are born, move and die before one can register them. New churches like the "Church of Jesus Christ" in Zone 9 draw people from other churches playing havoc with statistics. But to say that Guatemala is 30% evangelical is an accurate estimate.

The Background Makes the Difference

To know Latin America's Gospel People requires reviewing backgrounds — historical, political, social and economic. To know their religious history is to appreciate the tears, the pain and the courage of the early pioneers. To know their poverty is to understand people's search for meaning, for comfort, for relief and healing in evangelical communities. To witness their faith in action is to love them and better understand why Latin America's landscape is changing because of the Gospel People.

The story of Latin America's Gospel People is woven into the description of five waves of evangelical advance: (1) the early immigrant churches, (2) the mainline denominations, (3) the "faith missions," (4) the newer denominations, and (5) the churches sprouting from the soil of Latin America itself. Because the background *does* make a difference, the region's history, the current social and political situation and events in the Roman Catholic Church all form part of the picture that we paint.

CHAPTER TWO

Contradictory conquest

Francisco Pizarro and a handful of Spanish soldiers scaled the rugged Andes Mountains to the lofty atmosphere of Cajamarca in what is now northern Peru, and encountered the Inca emperor enjoying the baths in the town's hot springs. The plaza still stands where the Spanish conqueror had his chaplain read to the Indian the prescribed *requirimiento*, a formal demand to accept Christianity as well as to submit to the authority of the Pope and the Spanish crown.

Behind the *requirimiento* was a spirit of religious conquest which had been ordained, the conquerors felt, by God. 1492 was not only the year of Columbus's arrival in America, but also the year when seven centuries of fending off the Mohammedan Moors ended with the expulsion of the last infidel from Spanish soil. Were not all the riches of the New World a reward for Spanish tenacity in repelling the tide of Islam and thereby keeping all of Europe Christian?

There had been debates about whether the New World's Indians were human or animal. If they were human, Spain had an evangelistic responsibility towards them. One argument against their humanity was the fact that the Bible never mentioned them. But in defense of their humanity another argument pointed to the fact that Indians could laugh. Only humans had a sense of humor. This argument seemed convincing. So along with the prize of the New World came the responsibility to evangelize the native peoples.

Evangelization, Spanish Style

"Five Hundred Years of Evangelization" is the slogan of the Roman Catholic Church celebrating the anniversary of the Spanish and Portuguese conquest. Evangelization? To evangelical ears today the word seems out of place when it refers to the imposition of Roman Catholicism on the New World. It sounds stranger still when it embraces the mixture of military force with the reading of the *requirimientos* — a mix often quoted as symbolic of the conquest: *the Cross and the Sword.*

Some who look positively at Spain's "evangelization" even attribute special meaning to Columbus's name — *Christopher,* the "Christ-bearer" — the one who brought Christ to the New World.

A kind of black legend has been created concerning the conquest and the colonial period which followed that blinds us from seeing what an amazing achievement this was: Christianizing almost an entire hemisphere, superficial and unevangelical though we may now consider it to be.

Drive over a crest in Mexico and below will appear a broad valley with the sun reflecting off the shiny, tiled domes of the churches in every town. How did the conquerors manage to mobilize the human and material resources to build these massive stone cathedrals, the convents, the monasteries, shrines, seminaries and schools? In one town, Cholula, an Indian religious center, the conquerors built a church upon the site of every former pagan temple — a church for every day in the year, some claim. Actually there are only 77 in the vicinity — a remarkable number, nevertheless.

The British failed in India and the Dutch in Indonesia, to do what the Spanish and Portuguese did in Christianizing the Western Hemisphere. Even the pilgrims in Massachusetts, as religious as they were, did not establish as one of their primary purposes the evangelization of the native peoples.

Crosses and Glass Coffins

Place-names, Biblical expressions in everyday language ("God willing we'll meet on Friday"), Catholic religious education in the public schools in many countries, a monumental cross or figure of Christ presiding over a city from a nearby dominating mountain, feast days and processions filling the calendar — all attest to the penetration of a

Proud monuments of the 16th century Spanish "evangelization" — Mexico City's cathedral and the ancient Church of Antigua, Guatemala

degree of Christianity into the life and culture of a civilization that stretched from present-day San Francisco to Tierra del Fuego at South America's tip.

A Good Friday funeral procession commemorating Christ's death is still witnessed by weeping, black-shawled women. The municipal band plays a dirge. Costumed Roman soldiers march by as the glass coffin with its image of the dead Savior is carried slowly on the

shoulders of sober-faced pall bearers into the cathedral. The bell tolls as the afternoon shadows lengthen. The Latin soul is shaped by these events.

Was it only force that held Latin Americans to Christian forms through the centuries? In Paraguay, Indians were forced into the Jesuits' *misiones*, totalitarian colonial communities where the natives were taught trades and pressed into unbelievably regimented lifestyles. When the priests had to abandon the *misiones*, the Guarani Indians faded into the jungle. In this case, Christianization did not take.

But in Mexico, when a secular, revolutionary government, in conflict with the Church, tried to suppress religious activity, the pro-Catholic forces, the *Cristeros*, rebelled and laid down their lives in a vain attempt to overthrow the government. Graham Greene's novel *The Power and the Glory* portrays this remarkable era of Mexican history. A faith, with all its limitations, had penetrated.

The settlers on the North American coasts are often compared with the Latin American *conquistadores* ("the conquerors"). The pilgrims brought their families to settle in Massachusetts. In Latin America, however, the men came alone, without their families, to plunder a continent. To these, the Indian women proved attractive; the Spanish-Indian progeny became a new race, the *mestizo*. On the other hand, the European colonials in North America and elsewhere generally kept their distance from native populations. The Latin American conquest resulted in greater mixing. And evangelization, while often accompanied by the sword, was also accomplished by such racial mixing, many Indian peoples absorbing Christianity as they were absorbed in marriage or common-law union with the conquerors.

A Head Start for the Gospel

What does this history mean for us as we look at today's growth of the Gospel People? Does it simply point to Latin America's medieval Roman Catholicism to justify Protestant evangelism? As unevangelical and medieval as much of the region's traditional religion was, it nevertheless provided people with basic concepts about a Judeo-Christian faith. Catholics know who Mary, Christ and the apostles were. Though not often read, the Bible is respected. Though not always practiced, a Christian ethic is recognized and an appeal to conscience can be made. Even the Spanish *requirimiento* prepared the way for the Gospel People centuries later.

SUGGESTED FURTHER READING:

- George Pendle *A History of Latin America* (Viking—Penguin—Books of New York, 1973). This excellent brief history has been subsequently revised and updated in its many reprintings.

- William B. Prescott *The Conquest of Mexico Bound with The Conquest of Peru* (Modern Library of New York, 1931). A classic work on the Spanish conquest of the Aztec and the Inca empires.

- Graham Greene *The Power and the Glory* (Viking—Penguin—Books of New York, originally 1940).

CHAPTER THREE

Underside of glory

Pizarro's chaplain offered to Atahualpa, the Inca emperor, a book (a Bible or a missal), something the illiterate emperor had never seen before since the Incas had no written language. Even had he been literate, the book was in a foreign language, probably Latin. "God speaks to you through this book," said the priest. The emperor lifted it to his ear and heard nothing — an excellent example of cross-cultural non-communication — so he threw it to the ground. This constituted a signal for Pizarro's soldiers to attack, taking Atahualpa prisoner and demanding that gold be brought from all parts of the realm to fill a room to the level of a mark high on the wall. The mark and the wall still exist. Although he satisfied their demands, the emperor was murdered.

The extraordinary courage of Pizarro in Peru and Cortez in Mexico has to be seen also from the underside. It has its dark vignettes. A Caribbean chieftain refused to accept Christianity moments before his execution because if accepting Christ meant going to a heaven where rapacious Christians were, he wanted no part of it. As Indians were enslaved, abused and fell victim to European diseases, the estimated population of what is now Mexico declined from 7 million to 2 million by 1600.

A few voices were raised in protest. The most notable dissenter was Bartolomé de las Casas, whose footsteps are traced to what is now the Dominican Republic, Venezuela, Guatemala and Mexico. Priests of his stature were harassed by landowners, government officials and mine operators.

Spain's monopoly over commerce — trade was permitted only

with the mother country — was extended to thought and religion. Only certain books were authorized. In the Inquisition palaces of Cartagena, Lima and Mexico City, punishment was inflicted upon the heretic, be he the Jew, the hapless Lutheran sailor washed up on the shores of the Spanish Main or someone found selling a proscribed book.

Spanish inquisition scene

St. Ignatius Sí, Reformers No

In Cuzco, Peru, the Jesuit Church of the *Compañía*, like all colonial buildings in the city, rests upon ancient Inca foundations, clearly supplanting an earlier culture and religion. But the new faith was as totalitarian as the old. Just inside the door, on the inner wall, is a mural depicting St. Ignatius, the Jesuit founder, reading from his "Spiritual Exercises". Clearly identified at his feet in utter consternation are Luther, Calvin, Huss and other reformers. The Protestant Reformation never touched Spain and Portugal significantly, or the Iberian colonies.

John Mackay, in his classic *The Other Spanish Christ*, makes a point that the Christ of the Spanish mystics — Saint Teresa of Avila, Saint John of the Cross and others — was never taken to Latin America. These were to be sure, Catholics, but they were certainly saints who in the midst of medieval darkness discovered the presence of Christ. But their Christ never reached America — only the Christ of the *conquistadores*. The other Christ was left behind.

The Christ of the Conquerors of the New World is found in the dark corner of many a Catholic church — the bleeding, supine form in that glass coffin that will be carried in the streets on Good Friday. He is a battered, helpless Christ in the arms of Mary, as in the oft-reproduced sculpture, La Pieta. He elicits sorrow and pity, while Mary, tender-eyed and compassionate, draws one to solicit her mediation before God. *María nos lleva a Jesús* ("Mary leads us to Jesus") is a sticker seen in the windows of homes and cars. And until only a few years ago the admonition against reading the Bible was supported by the warning: "You'll go insane if you do."

Protestants were not much more successful in importing Christianity into the Iberian territories. Scattered attempts at Protestant colonization on the coasts of Venezuela and Brazil failed. Some formerly Spanish colonies became Protestant, but only because, as in the case of Jamaica, the British occupied the island by force.

Protestants Still Suspicious

Why should we remind ourselves of the history of dark religious totalitarianism in today's enlightened world? In many respects Catholicism has changed. The cities of Latin America are increasingly secular. One country, Uruguay, is so proudly secular that it has eliminated Christmas along with other religious holidays. But the fact remains that most of Latin America's five centuries of history were marked by a pre-reformation Catholicism that is not easily dismissed.

Even today, when a missionary reports that in a rural Mexican town a Protestant has been martyred for his faith, one should not be surprised. The Gospel People do not relate as easily to the Catholic Church as Protestants do in North America. The older generation of evangelicals may still remember how they personally were pursued by a fanatical mob and perhaps with the inciting priest holding a pistol. By the same token, older Catholics in Latin America still find accepting Protestants unsettling.

Catholic-Protestant tensions are accompanied by other concerns for the missionary.

A mixture of pagan rites and catholic worship within the Church of Chichicastenango, Guatemala

Contradictions and Credulity

An Indian sacrifices a chicken on the steps of the church in Chichicastenango, Guatemala, as tourists take pictures. Shrines built over pagan temples lead many observers to question how much the Indian may be directing his prayers to the ancient deity even though the image is that of a Christian saint. *Syncretism* — the mix of two religions — is no small concern for the missionary in the more primitive areas.

The distance between faith and practice is another concern. How can a belief so permeate a culture and people's emotions, even approach fanaticism, and yet not reach into the *personal and social ethics* of a society? Yesterday it was the conqueror raping the Indian. Today it is the dentist at the beach with his "other woman" and her children. Yesterday the colonizers drove the Indians into the silver mines. Today death squads kill union organizers in El Salvador.

Another concern is *popular religiosity* — non-formal practices that accrue around a creed that can become a substitute for real faith. There is a great gulf between the lofty theological and philosophical perspectives of St. Augustine and Thomas Aquinas and the old woman pasting crosses cut out of brown wrapping paper every two steps on the pavement. Or the miraculous medals. Or shuffling down the aisle of the church on one's knees. Form replaces substance in Latin America's folk religion.

For many people it is easy to believe the Virgin appeared in someone's back yard. Neighbors and TV crews stand around, hoping to see the miracle replicated. It is easy, too, to believe in a political demagogue. The fact that it is easy for the Latin American to believe — call it *credulity* — is not always bad. In contrast to the rational skepticism of the European or the North American, how wonderful it is to see credulity — in the best sense of the word — turned to the true object of faith, to Christ, the Savior. Faith in Christ comes easier in many cases for the Latin American.

This openness is another reason for the rapid numerical growth of the Gospel People.

SUGGESTED FURTHER READING:

- Enrique Dussel *A History of the Church in Latin America: Colonialism to Liberation* (Eerdmans of Grand Rapids, 1961). A Roman Catholic historian's view, from a perspective of Liberation Theology.

- John Mackay *The Other Spanish Christ* (Macmillan Company of New York, 1933). A classic study contrasting the faith of the conquerors with the deeper, mystical faith of some of the Spanish mystics. The book has been long out of print, but may be available in some libraries.

CHAPTER FOUR

Protestants and modernization

When the winds of independence began blowing in New England, the Anglicans (or Episcopalians), tied to the Church of England, were caught in an awkward position, with their loyalties attached to a church that was part of the colonial establishment. Some found themselves sabotaging the revolution; others fled to Canada.

In far more disarray was the Catholic Church in Latin America, when, in the 1820s, wars of independence broke ties with Spain. The links between the Church and the Mother Country included the Crown's right to appoint bishops in the New World. So the Church and the clergy, loyal to the Spanish king, found themselves on the wrong side of the conflict, except for a few priests, like Miguel Hidalgo y Costilla, who rang the bell that sparked the Mexican independence movement.

The new republics wanted to pick up the *patronato*, the right to appoint bishops, and, in effect, to control the Church, but the Pope had not given them this authority. There was confusion in the countries where deceased bishops had to be replaced and the lack of authority to make new appointments. It took years to unravel the situation.

The high walls which the colonial powers had erected crumbled under the impact of independence. And the outside world, with its systems of philosophy, education and government, came into full view. Books from new sources began to appear. But at first nothing as drastic as a change of religion was even considered. It was unthinkable to open up the region to the religion of the dreaded British pirates who had ravaged their coasts. The institutional church was in shambles, but a totalitarian religious view still prevailed.

Enthusiasm for the Bible

Like the Old Testament figure Melchizedek, or an unexpected comet in the night sky, the lone figure of Diego Thomson appeared in colonial America — first in Buenos Aires, then in Lima, and later in Bogotá, Colombia. Thomson, a Baptist, arrived in 1817, and soon began establishing Lancasterian schools. In this innovative approach to education, the more advanced pupils taught the younger ones, while reinforcing the lesson content for themselves. The Bible was one of the textbooks. Thomson was widely honored and decorated for his program. But he was also a missionary, organizing Bible societies for Scripture distribution.

Notable intellectuals, including some Catholic priests with a profound admiration for the Scriptures, formed part of these societies. Did Thomson have a strategy to plant Protestant churches later? There is no evidence of this. His goal seems to have been that of trusting that God's Word alone would effect the necessary changes, transform lives and reform the church from within.

God's Word will not return void. The Holy Spirit touched some hearts through the hundreds of Bibles distributed and eagerly read. But many a reader may have been like the Ethiopian (Acts 8) who read the Word but needed someone to explain it and, more than that, to demonstrate in real life the transforming power of God. There was no Luther versus Eck confrontation, as when the Protestant reformer debated with the Catholic hierarchy. Thomson was not expelled from Latin America. The effort simply evaporated and the Church, for the most part, continued to keep the Bible closed to its followers. The time was not ripe for reform within the Catholic Church.

The question is still raised: Why Protestant missions in Latin America? Why cannot the Catholic Church simply reform? The question was implied in the 1910 Edinburgh world missionary conference when Latin America was dismissed from consideration as a mission field. In contrast to Africa and Asia, the region was already "Christian". The question is even more relevant today, when the Catholic Church since Vatican II has seemingly grown more tolerant and even evangelistic. In many places it is distributing the Scriptures, and there are clearly regenerate people among its laity and clergy.

One reply to the question "Why Protestant missions?" is the fact that in many places the reforms have taken place in the presence of a vital and active evangelical church, as the older church was stimulated to look more seriously at the Scriptures as well as to adopt some Protestant forms and practices.

Then, in the 19th century, a new force appeared that began to open the door for the gospel.

British Locomotives, Southern Sugar Barons

Latin American liberals began to see in northern Europe a model for Latin America. These Latin intellectuals would be the free enterprise capitalists of today, hardly liberal by current definitions. But they advocated free trade, in contrast to the existing monopolistic economic patterns. And as "radical" liberals they pressed for secular government schools, instead of the church-controlled education of the colonial era.

In a race to catch up with the developed northern nations, there sometimes were slavish imitations — the downtown post offices of Mexico City and Santiago, Chile, are replicas of European public buildings a hundred years ago. The list of beaux arte opera houses and other imitations must certainly include the miniature Eiffel tower in Guatemala City.

As the liberals came into power now and again, they encouraged immigration from the advanced countries of the North to modernize Latin America.

Many a Latin American railroad keeps to the left, having been built by British engineers during the 19th century. In some Brazilian and Chilean towns, the German "Guten Morgen," is still more common than "Buenos días" or "Bom día" in Portuguese.

U.S. Southerners also came during the period when the institution of slavery was being questioned. These expatriates could not imagine a slaveless economy, so they went to Brazil, which still allowed slavery. The Brazilian city of Americana, named for the Americans who established sugar plantations in the area, has an American cemetery graced by an obelisk with a facing of colored tiles that form the pattern of the flag of the Southern Confederacy.

Welcoming these hardworking foreigners with their technology meant allowing them the right to practice their religion. The British established their Anglican churches and the Germans their Lutheran schools. Reluctantly, the door of religious freedom edged open. Though barely a ripple, these churches comprised the *first wave* of Protestant advance into Latin America.

An old "Cemetery for Foreigners" in many Latin American cities

The Good Shepherd Church (Episcopalian), first Protestant church in Costa Rica

reminds us that even in death the Latin Americans held these Protestant immigrants at a distance. The sacred soil of the cemeteries blessed by the Catholic Church was not available to heretics; theirs was the Potters's Field.

Foreigners Worshiping in Their Ghettos—Usually

In life, too, many immigrants kept apart from local society. Maps of many large Latin cities today still identify the locations of the Syrian Club, the British School and the German Lutheran church where a shrill pipe organ plays Bach and the pastor, imported from Europe, attends to the German community. Today, Americans of the mainline denominations, rather than establishing separate English-speaking denominations, worship together with other expatriates in "Union Churches" in every large city.

In many cases these "chaplaincy" ministries to the foreign communities were the first permanent Protestant witness in a country. While they usually limited themselves to their respective ethnic minorities, there are cases, more recently, where their witness reached outside their congregations.

An English-speaking Baptist church in the former Panama Canal Zone encouraged its members and friends to buy up a local radio station, HOXO, which became part of Latin America's network of evangelical stations.

Latvian immigrants to Brazil felt a responsibility for evangelizing Indians further inland, bought land and moved to Bolivia, and have faithfully witnessed in a place colorfully named *Rincón del Tigre* ("The Tiger's Corner").

When God does something exciting in a foreign community, local people standing around the edges may often call for a similar ministry in their own language. The Union Church of Monterrey, Mexico, had a vital outreach, and in response to Mexican interest, the pastor's son, Roger Wolcott, started a ministry in Spanish. This became a large evangelical congregation and training center. The project was named the "Castle of the King", having acquired a castle-like building on the edge of town originally constructed by an eccentric foreign mining engineer.

But such developments are usually recent. This initial immigrant wave of churches in the 19th century served their foreign communities and laid precedents for religious freedom for the succeeding waves of evangelical witness.

SUGGESTED FURTHER READING:

- J. Edwin Orr *Evangelical Awakenings in Latin America* (Bethany Press of Minneapolis, 1978). An excellent short history of Protestant work in Latin America. It covers more than the periods of revival.

CHAPTER FIVE

Gothic jewels and humble storefronts

The bitterly cold and desolate islands of Patagonia in southern Chile and Argentina were the goal of Allen Gardiner and his party. Forbidden to invade already "Christianized" populations, these English missionaries hoped to evangelize the Indians there. Follow-up supplies from England failed to arrive in time and the group died of starvation. A second group that arrived to replace them, including Gardiner's son, was wiped out in 1854 by the natives.

Other Dutch and French Protestant colonies tried to establish bridge-heads in Brazil during the Colonial period, but were driven off the land.

The Moravians from Europe were among the first Protestants to reach some of the Caribbean shores, coming not as missionaries who might return after several terms of service, but rather as permanent settlers to live and die in Latin America with a primary purpose of sharing the Gospel. The Atlantic coast of Nicaragua and Honduras, for example, became predominantly Protestant because of these Moravian settlements.

Part of the earliest U.S. witness was in the form of Bibles left by American soldiers who invaded Mexico. After the American West became populated, with churches in every frontier town, the attention of the mainline U.S. denominations could be directed towards Latin America.

Wanted: A Protestant Work Ethic and English Classes

Meanwhile, the Latin Americans with liberal political and economic views, many of them Free-Masons, went farther in their zeal for development. They suggested that even Protestant missionaries might be good for their countries. Such missionaries could introduce their schools, plus their Protestant values of hard work and a disciplined life. One suspects this might also have been a move to give the priests something to think about — at least a counterforce to check the power of the bishops. President Justo Rufino Barrios of Guatemala personally escorted the first Protestant missionary into the country in 1882, on his return by ship from a trip to the United States.

In the cities, European-style Protestant chapels were often erected. These Gothic jewels contrasted with the surrounding architecture. Some have long since disappeared, like Panama's Malecón (Seawall) Methodist Church, built on a pier over the harbor. Some have been relocated. But in many cities these century-old monuments with their varnished pews and commemorative plaques bear testimony to the pioneer missionaries who constructed them, and who were the precursors of the *second wave* of Protestant advance, the coming of the historical denominations. Except for missionaries who entered Argentina, Brazil, and Uruguay earlier, this wave washed Latin America's shores in the second half of the 19th century.

An understanding among the denominations ("comity" agreements) assigned, for example, the Presbyterians to Colombia and the Baptists to El Salvador. Larger countries were partitioned to accommodate various denominations.

Liberal-minded Latin Americans wanted progressive schools, free from the catechisms and rigid educational methods of the Catholic-dominated institutions. They promised to send their children to such schools if missionaries established them. So, in addition to the missionaries' own concern for the educational needs of the countries, mission schools seemed to be an appropriate means to reach the people.

The reputation of the schools grew as they expanded, some of them in Cuba and Brazil becoming universities. Missionaries found themselves caught up in the educational and administrative process. Local teachers, often non-evangelicals, had to be employed to meet government requirements — only local citizens could teach the country's history — and to fill the needs of an expanding curriculum. There just were not enough missionaries to go around.

A growing middle class was delighted to find a bilingual school or at least one with a good dose of English with North American teachers. Evangelical parents balked at sending children to public schools where religion classes were catechism studies and attendance at mass was obligatory.

While mission schools helped meet the tremendous educational needs of Latin America, relatively few of the new believers in the churches entered as a result of the schools. Thousands of graduates, however, became *simpatizantes* (friendly towards the Gospel). Many became forces for good in their society. Some, as government officials, rendered an occasional favor for the evangelical cause. Some schools which began as contributors to the community in loving service came to be mere self-serving institutions. Local teachers had to be paid, and tuition had to be charged. In effect they became elite private schools, less likely to be serving the social classes needing the most help.

These denominational churches and schools reflected the theological ebb and flow of their homeland churches, when, in the 20th century, the currents of skepticism and liberal theology began to make their impact. But on the whole they were more conservative theologically than their parent groups. More liberal elements tended not to consider Latin America as a mission field, which after all, was more Christianized than other continents.

Isn't Latin America "Christian"?

When the 1910 Edinburgh congress dismissed Latin America as a mission field, missionary leaders south of the border representing the major Protestant denominations met in Panama in 1916 for their own congress. They reaffirmed the region's need of the gospel, arguing that Latin America needed to be evangelized.

Some spiritual giants were the product of this second missionary wave. Gonzalo Báez-Camargo, a Mexican Methodist, fought in the Mexican revolution and then became a prolific writer, displaying a love for his country along with a defense of the Gospel. Whether working on an easy-to-read Spanish version of the Bible or defending Wycliffe Bible Translators in his newspaper column, he was one of

several Christian gentlemen-scholars who lent prestige to the Gospel
People.

But as some of the parent mainline denominations in the U.S.
began to suffer the inroads of theological liberalism, parts of the work
in Latin America began to slow down. In many a major city the old
downtown "First" church lost its fire. Newer and more aggressive
missionary groups entering a country in the first half of the 20th
century, not wishing to compete and finding the cities too expensive
and uncomfortable to live in, by-passed the cities and moved to rural
areas. This left major urban centers relatively unattended for decades.

Sometimes the Latin American daughter churches of the main-line
groups continued to be evangelistic while the North American parent
denomination was becoming liberal. This caused some zealous Latin
American daughter churches simply to fall out of step with the parent
denomination, and the ties between the two were broken.

Before the close of the 19th century, however, a new missionary
wave appeared on the horizon.

Gospel Tracts and Storefront Chapels

A new wave of men and women coming ashore in Latin America
represented the *third wave*, the "faith missions." Tim, an early proto-
type of these missionaries, quite likely came from a Minnesota farm.
When automobiles and tractors became more common, he developed
handyman skills. He was often more adept at fixing a carburetor or
nailing down corrugated iron roofing on a chapel than his better-
educated denominational missionary counterpart. Tim's books rested
on boards-and-brick shelving. Until he could get around to making a
table, his lamp stood on a proverbial missionary barrel disguised with
colorful draping. His wife met regularly for coffee with other wives,
often to discuss their perennial maid problems. From more sheltered
backgrounds, none of them had faced before questions such as what to
do with the maid's illegitimate baby or alcoholic brother, or the
irritant of her family continually pressing for loans or her boy friend at
the gate every evening.

These enthusiastic young people of the faith mission movement
traced the origins of their missionary ministry to Hudson Taylor, who
was called by God to serve in inland China. Denominational leaders
would not permit Taylor to start a work in the interior. Nonetheless, he

found friends to support him financially, so without the sponsorship of a denomination, in faith he set out under the nondenominational society he founded — China Inland Mission (now Overseas Missionary Fellowship).

There were other reasons for the rise of faith missions. With a loss of confidence by many in the theology of the mainline denominations and their respective missions, thousands of more conservative Christians found a vehicle for their missionary outreach in such societies as CAM International (originally the Central American Mission, founded by C. I. Scofield of the dispensational Scofield Bible) or TEAM (The Evangelical Alliance Mission). The first CAM couple went to Central America in 1891. A greater number of "faith missionaries" arrived when the modernist-fundamentalist controversy peaked in the 1920s and 1930s.

The missionaries of this wave tended to be graduates of the Bible Institute movement. The churches they planted started modestly in their own living rooms, in a new believer's home or in a storefront. Tracts and simple literature were printed and a Bible school (with a curriculum adapted from the missionary's alma mater) was initiated in the back of the church. Radio was utilized when it became available.

Stones sometimes clattered on the tin roofs, thrown by fanatical neighbors. There were confrontations with priests when the missionary first visited a village. In Tim's case, his wife played the portable pump organ. Tim followed with a simple message, preached with a traditional invitation for the few listeners to respond. Gradually children and then adults began to fill the crude pews.

More than once, missionaries were stranded when their faith supporters failed them. Despite failures and setbacks, however, the faith mission wave touched the length and breadth of Latin America. One mission specialized in radio. The World Radio Missionary Fellowship established the first missionary radio station, HCJB, in Quito, Ecuador, when the country had only a handful of people with receivers. Another, the Latin American Evangelization Campaign (later, the Latin America Mission) began in 1921 by conducting citywide united evangelistic campaigns. Wycliffe Bible Translators and New Tribes Mission reached Indian populations in the jungles and in the mountains.

Money for Missionaries, Not for Missions

When Tim found that young Felipe was an excellent prospect for further theological training, or that Mario needed a modest salary so that he could use his gifts to start new churches, or when Tim awoke to the need for funds to print a Bible study book, a problem arose. The faith mission structure leaned heavily on personal contact between the missionary and his North American donor friends. People in Mankato, Minnesota, were all too happy to buy Tim a jeep or contribute to his family's financial support. But their enthusiasm did not transfer easily to Felipe and Mario.

National believers often wondered why it was so hard to raise funds to print a book or get a scholarship. The denominations apparently had a freer hand to allocate funds and had more resources; everything was not so tightly linked to the missionary. Faith missions had money available for the Bible Institute as long as the missionary was on the scene. It was therefore tempting to keep institutions under missionary control to assure their funding. Denominational institutions seemed less dependent on the missionary presence.

Despite these limitations, churches multiplied, radio stations installed larger transmitters and Bible institutes graduated thousands of

Left: a Gospel service in a tropical, rural setting in Colombia. Top: a store-front congregation in Peru. Below: a Costa Rican evangelical chapel — all three the results of "faith missions."

Latin American pastors and leaders.

Although Tim and his colleagues came from a variety of denominational backgrounds, there was surprisingly little argument about the kinds of churches to be produced on the field. Most practiced baptism by immersion and ended up with a congregational form of government. Although the mission boards were interdenominational, in each country the churches which they created soon formed associations and became new local denominations.

Succeeding generations of missionaries were more theologically sophisticated and national churches and pastors were given more say in field decisions. The movement became obviously more mature.

Despite shoestring budgets and simplistic theology, the faith mission wave turned out to be bigger, covering more of the beach. Each new wave of evangelical advance — this one and those yet to come — seemed to be bigger, but never obliterating the impressions made by the previous crests. Nor did the waves break in exactly the same order or with the same intensity on every shore. But the spectacular rise of the Gospel People in the last thirty years could not have taken place without the generations of lives spent in often discouraging and apparently fruitless evangelistic toil.

As the stage was getting set for an evangelical explosion many years later, the seeds of economic and political explosions were also being planted.

The Underside of Modernization

Investors discovered Latin America and built textile factories in Mexico, planted banana plantations in Honduras and established utility companies like the "Light, Power and Heat" electric company in Panama (which eventually dropped the "Heat" in its name, given Panama's torrid climate).

Modernization and economic infrastructures were necessary, but the human element was too frequently overlooked. Industrialization without concern for people created Latin American cities like the London described by Dickens and the U.S. factories portrayed later by Upton Sinclair. Major profits flowed out of the region instead of being retained to improve conditions.

The North produced a tycoon like Henry Ford, who, while keeping unions out of his factories nevertheless paid better than the going wage and created a charitable foundation. Carnegie built libraries. This was capitalism tempered by a modicum of Christian social responsibility.

By contrast, Latin American capitalism was ruthless, the wealthy contributing hardly a token for charity.

Reaction to soul-less modernization started soon. The Mexican Revolution early in the 20th century was not just a revolt against an aging dictator, Porfirio Díaz. It also was a revolt against a system that was modernizing the country at the expense of the people. Many Protestants took up arms on the side of the Revolution.

Throughout the region, difficulties increased during the depression years, and before any economic recovery could be enjoyed, World War II crashed upon the scene.

Nine countries quickly identified with the Allied cause. Legend has it that Hitler looked on the globe for tiny Costa Rica, when even before the U.S., it declared itself at war with the Axis; but his finger was covering the spot.

In some countries Germans were herded into prison camps or returned to Germany. In a few South American countries with a goose-stepping military tradition, sympathy towards the Axis prevailed. Argentina, for example, did not declare war until 1945 when the Axis defeat was certain.

German and Italian airlines were confiscated. The U.S. built air bases and used Brazilian fields to ferry planes across the Atlantic. Axis submarines roamed the coastal areas making travel on the high seas dangerous. Latin America's petroleum and other products for the war took priority on the sea lanes. Shortages boosted prices and missionary activity was reduced to a minimum.

But the dark parenthesis of the war years was but a prelude to what would be the brighter years to come.

CHAPTER SIX

Years of optimism

C. P. Snow in his novel, *The New Man*, records the remark of a cynical British journalist when confronted with the dawn of universal history. Western Europe would no longer be center stage. Said Snow: "The party's nearly over. The party for our kind of people, for dear old Western man — it's been a good party, but the host's getting impatient and it's nearly time to go."

The years following World War II ushered in a new spirit of expectation and optimism throughout the world. The horrible war was over. The evil of war, however necessary it may have been, was now past history. In its wake a world revolution was in the making in all areas of life. Technological, social, economic, political and religious structures were about to be drastically altered.

New flags were unfurled and raised as new nations in Africa and Asia were born. The colonial yoke was smashed. These brand new states launched into an exciting if sometimes precarious existence, their peoples imbued with a new sense of awareness and a new-found faith in the future. With this came the perception by some that we were witnessing the death throes of Western civilizations.

However, in the post-war era the U.S. emerged as the great Western world power. As the U.S. became engaged immediately in the bitter Cold War with the Communist regimes, there was a continuing awareness of its power and mission to fend off the Communist menace. With the nuclear bomb came atomic energy for commercial purposes.

The U.S. had the dollars — or at least could borrow on its future — to carry out its post-war dreams. The incredible Marshall Plan to restore the countries of western Europe, including West Germany, was a dramatic indication of Yankee initiative.

This was a time to reap the fruit of technology, much of it the result of invention and development during the war. There was a quantum leap in every area: in communications, from the AM radio era to FM and TV; in transportation, from piston engine planes to jets; in arms, from conventional explosives to atom bombs. There were rapid strides in the field of metallurgy. And new products such as ballpoint pens, dacron cloth, nylon rope, and plastics appeared on the market. These advances quickly penetrated to the far corners of the world.

Latin America Joins the Global Village

It was not uncommon even in the middle 1950s to see a barefoot *campesino* (peasant) trudging off to work in the coffee groves with a machete belted to his side and a transistor radio held fast to his ear. The transistor exposed "common folk" to an overwhelmingly new world.

The global network of mass media (press, radio, film and TV) fanned new desires all over the world. As a result, public opinion came to be a factor in the world arena. Latin Americans joined the throng, although in the first 20 post-war years, UNESCO studies showed that several Latin American countries fell below the world-wide mass media standard.

There was a positive attitude abroad as modernization ground on in the Latin republics. Perhaps more optimism exuded from U.S. expectations about what should happen there, than from Latin citizens themselves. However, the modernization process, primarily involving urbanization, literacy, and use of mass media, lurched forward.

With the increase of air travel, Latin America was suddenly nearer to the U.S. Up to 1958, piston-powered flights from Los Angeles to Costa Rica still took about 24 hours of a passenger's time — first an all-night flight from Los Angeles to Guatemala City, an 8-hour layover, and then the "milk-run" through every Central American capital.

Even this arduous trip was faster than the previous "banana boat" voyages to a Costa Rican coastal port, still some three hours from the capital city, San José. Jet flight has, of course, accelerated travel even more. Latin America became readily accessible to tourists seeking sunny Caribbean beaches or eager to explore Mayan pyramids.

A Friend in the White House

The optimism of the age pervaded U.S. sentiment towards Latin America. It was felt that future peace and freedom in Latin America were dependent on understanding by both governments and individuals. Furthermore, Communism had to be checked. An attack on Vice President Richard Nixon's automobile in Venezuela in 1958 awakened many North Americans to anti-Americanism south of the border. The event was generally blamed on Communist protest.

Outstanding and most ambitious of optimistic efforts by the U.S. was the *Alliance for Progress*, a fresh attempt to replace the outworn *Good Neighbor* policy of the Roosevelt era. It was launched at the Punta del Este Conference in Uruguay in August of 1961, not any too soon, given the fact that by then Cuba was considered already lost to democracy and there was chilling fear of "more Cubas."

Earlier that year, President John F. Kennedy had proposed the concept to Latin American representatives at the White House. Kennedy enjoyed unusual popularity in Latin America, not only for his youth and charisma, but also for the fact that he was the first U.S. Roman Catholic president. Many a Latin park or barrio bears his name.

The preamble of the Alliance for Progress charter begins enthusiastically:

" . . . we, the American Republics, hereby proclaim our decision to unite in a common effort to bring our people accelerated economic progress and broaden social justice within the framework of personal dignity and political liberty."

The Alliance covered a wide range of projects and programs in many fields. Each republic was to set its own domestic goals and do its own planning — of course, within the general framework of the Alliance. It embraced such far-flung areas in its objectives as:

- priority to projects in less-developed countries to achieve a measure of equality in living standards;
- agrarian reform;
- more equitable distribution of national income;
- utilization of natural resources and providing employment for unemployed and part-time workers;
- reduction of dependence on export of only a few primary products while raising agricultural productivity, storage, trans-

portation and marketing services;
* cooperative programs to prevent excess fluctuation in foreign exchange;
* formation of Latin American common markets;
* increase of construction of low-cost housing;
* elimination of adult illiteracy and notable improvement of all educational systems;
* increased life expectancy by improvement of health standards and better water quality and sewage disposal.

One of the major issues of the program was the need to get the great masses of the "poorest of the poor" (those living on less than $100 a year) to support the Alliance. Hooked in with this objective was the need to overcome the causes of poverty in many places, such as: natural resource deficiencies in the 19 smaller countries, the "half-primitive" economies, the insecurity, the ineffective government, and the population explosion, estimated at an annual rate of 2.6 to 2.9% in 1962.

Brazilian Beetles and Malarial Mosquitos

In the spirit of the time, the Alliance for Progress was ·hailed as a major force in removing poverty and underdevelopment. It also paved the way for private investment. Governments granted concessions for oil drilling in Ecuador. Factories mass-producing VW "Beetles" sprouted in Mexico and Brazil.

Productivity on the farm increased by three or four times through the *Green Revolution*, which employed new hybrid seeds, insecticides and fertilizers.

Yellow fever had been licked in Latin America when the U.S. built the Panama Canal. Malaria was next to go. It was discovered that malarial mosquitos land only on vertical surfaces. Spraying the walls of people's houses with DDT was all that was necessary to wipe out the blight in vast low-land areas. Health cards indicating that one's small pox vaccinations were up-to-date had been part of every traveller's documentation upon entering an international airport. Eventually these were no longer required.

The benefits of what health officials call "primary health care" — such as clean drinking water, latrines, measures against intestinal parasites — meant lower death rates accompanied by exploding populations. Birth control was an obvious element in the package for Latin American progress. The Roman Catholic Church, while officially against birth control, has been remarkably silent in Latin America regarding the subject. It was often the political left that screamed birth control was a U.S. imperialist plot to weaken the Third World.

Other signs of progress and achievement appeared. One of the more visible was the Inter-American Highway, linking many of the region's capitals. It only lacked the link between Panama and Colombia to complete it. More license plates of cars and trucks from neighboring countries began to appear — a sign of increased trade and communication between countries. Regional trade was stimulated by efforts such as the Central American Common Market.

Other road networks, such as those penetrating the Amazon basin, opened up the interior of many countries whose major populations had long been hugging the coasts. Scenes reminiscent of the American Old West were revived as 20th century homesteaders followed the new roads and carved out new farm lands in the interior.

What Can We Do for You?

Major *inter-governmental organizations* sprang into existence, to foment regional unity and development. Many were related to the United Nations Organization, others to the U.S. government. A.I.D. (the Agency for International Development), E.C.L.A. (the U.N.'s Economic Commission for Latin America), and the O.A.S. (the Organization of American States, replacing the floundering Pan American Union) all played major roles in the total program.

The International Development Bank and the International Monetary Fund later became prominent as they offered economic aid to countries accepting their conditions.

Other demonstrations of U.S. will to help Latin America were the *various cultural exchange programs* and the *Peace Corps*. A third of the Corps' volunteers by 1962 had gone to twelve Latin American countries. After crash courses in Spanish, Corps volunteers, many of them idealistic back-packing U.S. young people, helped villages lay water pipes, taught trades, helped Latins start small businesses, taught school or directed recreational and sports programs.

What'd It All Mean?

The concept of progress and planning began to replace traditional Latin American fatalistic mind sets. Such things as literacy and agrarian reform led people to break out of their traditional ways of looking at things. Plans *can* be made. One *can* make decisions instead of being bound to *que será, será*, ("what will be, will be").

This kind of new thinking also meant that people would more likely be ready "to kick over the traces" and break from social mores. They would also be more open to listen to new ideas and even more readily receptive to the transforming power of the gospel of Jesus Christ.

More roads, speedier air travel, and better communications made it easier for Christian missions to enter and to evangelize. Migrations to the interior of some countries meant that people in more towns would be open to the "Good News." Other masses moving into cities where industrialization was taking place were likewise generally more receptive to the Christian message, having made a substantial break from their traditional rural social structure.

And yet, could it be that Protestant missionaries depended too much on technology and many favorable external circumstances? Were they not also infected unduly with the over-riding optimistic spirit of the age?

One thing was certain: the "old party" of colonization was over. Latin America — and the whole world for that matter — would never be quite the same again.

SUGGESTED FURTHER READING:

- W. Stanley Rycroft and Myrtle M. Clemmer *A Factual Study of Latin America* (New York: Office for Research, Commission on Ecumenical Mission and Relations, the United Presbyterian Church in the U.S.A., 1963). Excellent broad outline of the processes of change in the early 1960s in the demographic, political, economic, social, and religious patterns.

- Milton S. Eisenhower *The Wine Is Bitter: The United States and Latin America* (New York: Doubleday and Company, 1963). Fruit of eight years of study and analysis of Latin America, authorized by President Eisenhower, involving history of hemisphere relations, outline of program to stimulate Latin American growth, and underlining threat of "several other Castros."

- Salvador de Madariaga *Latin America Between the Eagle and the Bear* (New York: Frederick A. Praeger, 1962). He underscores enormous Communist infiltration among Latin intellectuals. Description and analysis of domestic causes, relationship between U.S. and Latin America and between Latin America and Soviet/Chinese with a simple plan of action for the U.S.

CHAPTER SEVEN

The Call for 40,000

We are told that in his last hours, even after he had received Extreme Unction, Pope John XXIII repeated many times, "Oh, the great work for Latin America." Each time his face was transformed with obvious satisfaction, and his hand traced a blessing in confirmation of his words.

Much later, however, U.S. Bishop John Fitzpatrick, commenting on the extraordinary efforts of the U.S. Catholic Church to help the Roman Church in Latin America, said in frustration: "We should have cased the joint before opening up a franchise."

In the early 1960s the Roman Catholic Church in the U.S. shared the optimistic mood of the day and carried out an unprecedented collective mission to Latin America. John Considine was the most vocal proponent of a massive effort to send misioners to the south. Estimating that 80 million Catholics of the region were without adequate pastoral care and, adopting a ratio of one priest for every 2000 people, he appealed for 40,000 to pack their bags and give Latin America a hand.

Why Padres from the U.S.?

Not only was there a lack of Catholic pastors in Latin America, but U.S. Catholics were concerned about the Communist threat as well, and the increase in Protestant growth in Latin America. Emboldened by the two Catholic world leaders — Pope John XXIII in the Vatican and President John Kennedy in the White House — and motivated by a sincere desire to help others, Catholics launched a gigantic program.

The CICOP (Catholic Inter-American Cooperation Program) sponsored discussions of church relations with Latin America. In general, U.S. Catholics knew little about their brothers and sisters in the south. They could not understand why the Latin Church could not support its own programs. "Why should we have to send priests when there are so many Latin Catholics down there?" So, CICOP provided a platform for presenting the cause.

Father Leo T. Mahon, head of an innovative parish among the poor in San Miguelito near Panama City and of the Latin American mission of the Archdiocese of Chicago, underlined the goals for the Roman Catholic Church in 20th Century Latin America which included: creating "family" (community) rather than mere organization; shaping social rather than merely individual conscience; building "church," rather than schools or even church buildings; and forming a committed, rather than just a knowledgeable, people.

But most of the grandiose effort put into this campaign did not reflect Mahon's perceptive outlook, especially in the earlier years. Rather, the program seemed caught up in the prevailing optimistic spirit of the age — a pragmatic, "do-it-now," American instant "know-how."

Actually, some efforts of North American Catholics to help the Latin Church began as early as 1946, in a seminar in Havana, Cuba. Delegates to the meeting were chosen by bishops in each country to study the social problems of the hemisphere. Two concerns rose quickly to the surface: the "considerable headway" made by evangelical Protestants and the Communists in Latin America.

The Society of St. James, enthusiastically backed by Cardinal Richard Cushing, played a major role in the effort, especially in providing a flood of missioners in the 1960s. The Cardinal's vision began with his visit to Pope Pius XII in 1945. The Society of St. James became synonymous with "saving Latin America from Communism."

In 1961, Monseignor Agostino Casaroli, a Vatican diplomat, delivered a speech at the University of Notre Dame, where he warned of the "inroads of Protestantism" and the "menace of Marxism" in Latin America. Contrasting the needs of the South with the riches of the U.S., he, too, called for more North American priests to minister in Latin America.

While Father John Considine called for 10% of the U.S. clergy to go as missioners to Latin America, Pope John was recruiting elsewhere, especially in France and Canada. Meanwhile, the Society of St. James picked up steam and between 1959 and 1962, due primarily to Cardinal Cushing's efforts, it recruited 70 priests.

The 1600 U.S. missioners in Latin America in 1950 increased by 50% to 2400 by 1960. The peak year was 1968, when 3391 were serving in the Latin world. In addition, there were 2000 Canadians by 1971. But Considine's 1946 goal of 40,000 was missed by a very wide margin.

Nevertheless, the Catholic effort was remarkable. Up to 1960 and the beginnings of the Second Vatican Council in the 1960s, U.S. bishops knew little about the Latin American Church.

The Downhill Trail

Gerald Costello poignantly describes the ending of this rather incredible movement as follows: [The U.S. missioners] " . . . were, many of them, the brightest hopes of the U.S. church of the sixties. Their special crusade began in the clear, hopeful days of John F. Kennedy, of armies for peace and alliances for progress, of a church that stood rock-firm, of a pope whose heart seemed big enough to hold the world. It ended quietly, in the gathering darkness of a fortress presidency and a troubled pope, a church that was offering options instead of answers, and a war in Vietnam that was tearing the U.S. apart." (*Mission to Latin America*, page 168).

What went wrong? Several specific factors can be cited from Roman Catholic sources, indicating the enterprise was doomed from the beginning.

1. The attitude of expecting to "do a big job in a hurry in Latin America," to be finished in 4 or 5 years, made for a woefully inadequate start. The U.S. bishops were extremely nationalistic, inward-looking, and traditional. "Foreign lands" were strictly for "missionaries," leaving no room to create a spirit of brotherhood with sisters and brothers of faith already there.

An old Peruvian put it well to a U.S. priest when he said, "Missioners came down with a full chalice, overflowing. Instead, they should have come with an empty cup. Then, we would have filled it with you."

2. There was no real grass-roots input from Latin America until late in the game, and only then haphazardly. Incredible as it seems, Latin American bishops were completely by-passed in the planning and

preparation of the venture.

In 1976, a Franciscan Father who had served in Honduras and El Salvador, stated: "Americans brought American know-how with them, but they didn't take into account the system already in use here. They had the idea that every parish had to have a rectory, a convent for sisters, a school, and a church. Then they began to build dispensaries, clinics, basketball courts, hospitals, roads, cooperatives — all necessary, but all American style. Very few took into account the native customs, systems, attitudes, management. The staff had to be U.S. if it were to succeed." (*Mission to Latin America*, page 50).

3. The recruiting of missionaries was not coordinated with the training and placement end. In the early years, no solid operational principle was established. Requests from Latin America were expected to come on a specific need basis. These needs were to be reflected in recruitment, training, and processing to the field, presumably with adequate cultural orientation and language acquisition.

But things got out of hand. Soon there were accepted candidates without places to go. New personnel were forced into places of service already full of missioners. As a result, more than 50% never fulfilled their 2-year promise. Certain areas bred ghetto-like concentrations of North Americans. Eventually, the Latin American bishops politely suggested that perhaps the situation and results proved not to be worth the effort.

Added to this placement difficulty were the nagging problems of missioner training. Central to much of the difficulty was the brilliant and controversial priest, Ivan Illich. He was appointed in 1961 to establish the Center of Intercultural Formation (later renamed the International Center of Documentation — CIOD) in Cuernavaca, Mexico, with the goal of training U.S. personnel assigned to Latin America.

"Shock treatment" and unorthodox Yankee-baiting methods left only 39 of the first 68 students, male and female, surviving the ordeal. These bizarre methods soon came to the attention of the U.S. Catholic public thus arousing a tempestuous relationship. The stormy Illich left active ministry in 1969 and in 1976, the Cuernavaca Center closed down.

4. There were differences between leaders regarding strategies and tactics. Much of this boiled down to superiors versus staff. Most of the bishops and religious hierarchy followed traditional lines, but a vocal

minority shared an increasingly radical approach to meeting Latin America's gigantic problems. John Considine was a traditionalist, while Illich and Colonnese led from the critics' corner. Father Frederick McGuire in the North, Panamanian Bishop Marcos McGrath and others got caught in the middle.

Actually, the heart of the matter was that this enterprise — conceived in the unexpected, executed in a hurry, and ultimately abandoned in futility — lacked a solid policy framework.

5. Following the General Conference of Latin American Bishops in Medellín, Colombia, in 1968, the waves of Liberation Theology began to sweep through the Latin American Catholic Church. The new focus on liberating people from capitalistic systems replaced the U.S. Catholic concept of development within the existing system.

In the Rearview Mirror

Roman Catholic sources candidly give low marks to their effort's achievements in evangelizing the people, fostering national vocations, and stemming the Communist threat.

One positive result. The effort assisted in the birth of a dynamic new Latin American church of the people. Because the outcome was not one of the original goals it is difficult to perceive how the Catholic missionary endeavor had much to do with it.

Mention could be made of the internationalizing effect on a large and influential number of the U.S. Catholics. The "primary beneficiary of the Latin American mission apostolate" was the sending church in the north. Some missioners took on the joys and sorrows of the *campesinos* (the peasants). One participant put it beautifully: "They taught us how to be human."

And so, the U.S. Catholic Church mission program, as such, ground to a halt in the 1970s.

Christ in Our Suitcases

"We should have cased the joint before opening up a franchise." Bishop Fitzpatrick's honest insight speaks to us all — U.S. Roman Catholics and U.S. evangelicals alike. Despite all of the admitted failures, some U.S. priests, nuns and lay workers blew new and fresh winds into the Latin American Roman Catholic Church. U.S.

Pope Paul in Bogotá in 1968.

Franciscans from Wisconsin, for example, serving on the east coast of Nicaragua, cooperated there with the Anglicans, Baptists and Moravians in bringing Anglican Bishop Festo Kevengere of Uganda for a cooperative evangelistic campaign.

Did this unusual continent-wide Catholic mission effort produce the greatly needed changes? Not at all. By the time it ground to a stop, the Latin church was different, but not because of the program. Other influences proved stronger. These will be considered in succeeding chapters.

This chunk of history speaks to the evangelical church as well. We are a long way from having done everything right in Latin America. And today we understand more clearly our failures and weaknesses by looking at this snapshot of Catholic history.

We can nod our heads knowingly at the failures of this Roman Catholic venture. But how much in-depth understanding do we have about Latin Americans and their real needs? Have we not also been all too eager to put into action simplistic, grandiose and foreign programs without really conferring with "the Protestant bishops"? How about our own attitudes of superiority and paternalism, our all-too-often inadequate orientation and language acquisition programs, and deficient pastoral care of our personnel?

Father John Gorski's words in 1976 ring clearly to all of us: "Missionaries have to avoid the thought that Christ comes down in their suitcases. If we really believe that Christ comes down before us, then we must first discover how the Holy Spirit is already present among the people."

There was no room for that concept in the early Catholic missions in Latin America, nor in the Catholic effort of the 1960s. All too often the Protestant missionary movement is also characterized by the same "suitcase mentality."

SUGGESTED FURTHER READING:

- Gerald M. Costello *Mission to Latin America (The Successes and Failures of a 20th Century Crusade)* (Orbis Books of Maryknoll, New York, 1979.) An entire book devoted to the missionary effort described in this chapter. Much of the material in this chapter has its source in this book.

- John G. Considine *The Call for 40,000* (Longmans, Green and Company of Toronto, 1946) A popular — now past history, of course — description of Roman Catholicism in Latin America in the post-war period with his appeal for a massive influx of U.S. personnel.

CHAPTER EIGHT

Ex-GI's, radio and airplanes

In January, 1956, the news flashed around the world that five U.S. missionaries had been killed by Auca spears in the jungle of eastern Ecuador. LIFE magazine picked up the story, not only for its human interest, but because it placed in juxtaposition primitive tribes and modern technology — the airplane, radio communications and other tools these missionaries had been using.

A few years earlier in 1951, representatives of evangelical radio stations in Ecuador, Costa Rica, Haiti, Guatemala and Panama met also in Ecuador to work out a scheme to exchange Christian radio programs, now that tape recordings had come on the scene. Subsequently similar stations sprouted up in Peru, Bolivia, in other Central American countries and the Caribbean islands.

The resulting Pan American Christian Network had its counterpart in LEAL, an organization of evangelical publishers and booksellers. The radio and literature organizations sponsored several communications congresses to promote the spread of the Gospel in the region.

Post-World War II classes in U.S. Christian colleges and seminaries were filled with ex-GI's (World War II veterans) who had seen for themselves the spiritual needs overseas. Those going to Latin America had been preceded by experienced missionaries from parts of the Orient — China and North Korea — which were closed by the war to missionary efforts. The post-war can-do optimism also infected evangelical missions.

Only a few years before, all of the Protestants in many a Latin city may not have filled one side of the soccer stadium. Now the numbers were increasing and large, united evangelistic campaigns could muster impressive crowds of *evangélicos* and their interested friends.

Early evangelical radio outreach in Central America

Billy Graham's 1958 "Caribbean Crusade" took him on a circuit of eight countries. In the years that followed many Latin American evangelists took to the crusade pulpits — Luis Palau, "Hermano Pablo" Finkenbinder, and Alberto Mottesi among others. Many international evangelists continue to serve significantly.

Perhaps more important than the number of decisions registered in a given crusade was the way the public became conscious of the gospel through these efforts. The Tommy Hicks healing campaign in Buenos Aires became the kind of event which everyone began talking about, and was unquestionably a benchmark of evangelical history in that country.

Added to the previous waves of evangelical advance in Latin America (the immigrant churches, the main-line denominations and the faith missions), a *fourth wave* began washing ashore during this post-war period: the new denominations.

A huge, silvery blimp-like enclosure supported by the higher air pressure inside, the "Air Cathedral", was used for a while by Assemblies of God missionaries in Central America. The modern equivalent of the old tent meeting approach, this represented the campaign emphasis of the post-war wave.

Traditional tents are still being used, too, for evangelistic campaigns. And the dry season in the tropics lends itself to open-air campaigns in large vacant lots. People still endure backless benches under strings of lights while they listen to a preacher present his message from a crude platform. The campaign may last three months, leaving a preacher hoarse and exhausted. Not many may respond on a given night. But if a total of 500 respond over a three month period and only 10% remain faithful, one still has a nucleus of 50 with which to begin a new church.

One such well-publicized "Great Healing Campaign" on the edge of San José, Costa Rica, eventually became a large Pentecostal church with a handsome building. But the name stuck; it is still popularly known as "La Gran Campaña" — the great campaign.

Not all missionaries of this fourth wave are Pentecostal: neither do all major in evangelistic campaigns. Conservatives of many of the old North American denominations despaired of regaining control of the organizations and the mission boards. Breaking away, new non-Pentecostal groups such as the Conservative Baptists or the more recently formed Presbyterian Church of America sent their missionaries south of the border with greater evangelistic fervor than the older denominations. Such groups were less inclined to have open-air campaigns than home Bible study groups.

Some of the older denominations, such as the Southern Baptists or the Mennonites, although already in Latin America, awoke to the needs in other countries and expanded their fields. The total number of missionaries of this wave and the previous one (faith missions) represented 90% of all North American missionary personnel overseas in 1989, and their proportion in Latin America was probably the same.

Already strong in countries like Brazil and Chile, Pentecostals entered new areas and attracted the most followers. They added prayer for the sick to the campaign approach and television to their media efforts. They replaced the piano and organ with electric guitars.

The rapid evolution in style even left some of the earlier Pentecostal groups behind. One denomination in Mexico almost looks like two denominations. The churches of an earlier period are small and tucked tightly between other buildings. An older generation sings from an out-of-print hymnal and has the evident air of a persecuted minority. In contrast, the newer churches of the same denomination are large and colorful with contemporary choruses played by what comes close to being a rock band.

In another country, the older generation rejected the younger missionaries, especially the North American women who sported current hair fashions, jewelry and cosmetics. The earlier missionaries and the churches they founded were decidedly more legalistic.

The joyous worship style, the clapping to the songs, the tambourines and the spontaneity, spread to traditional denominations even though many do not share Pentecostal doctrine. Baptist churches in Argentina and Presbyterians in Brazil and Venezuela found renewal in various degrees of charismatic involvement as they broke from forms that had grown sterile across the years. A movement of the Spirit among many churches in Buenos Aires in the late 1960s generated fresh Latin American hymns and choruses and new concepts of worship touching churches throughout the continent.

Large congregations created by the third wave — that of faith missions — were superseded in many cities by the Pentecostal churches of the fourth. The largest group in Mexico City holds continuous services all day long in a former winery. Another meets in a huge remodelled automobile sales center. The former creates new branch churches by encouraging hundreds of their members in the already-established churches to forgo meeting in their home church for several months in order to attend services in a new location and thus give the branch congregation a jump-start. Hundreds descend on the new location, perhaps a warehouse. The singing and excitement make an immediate impact on the neighborhood, attracting the curious. Within a few months there are enough local people involved so that others can return to their home churches. A large congregation is born almost instantaneously instead of starting at square one with a handful of people.

Getting Every Christian into the Act

Kenneth Strachan, former director of Latin America Mission, observed growing churches, Pentecostal and non-Pentecostal alike, well before church growth studies were formalized. For him, the most significant factor in church growth was *mobilization*, training and motivating all members of a church in continuous witness. This was the theoretical basis for the Evangelism-in-Depth movements coordinated by the LAM during the 1960s. In 10 countries year-long efforts were carried out, with the participation of nearly every evangelical denomination. The program included campaigns, special efforts to reach particular social groups and the widespread use of radio and literature. But central to each effort was the objective of training and encouraging every Christian to tell his or her friends about Christ.

The close of each effort was an evangelical parade in the capital city. And the euphoria of the thousands of believers carrying Bibles and singing as they marched down the streets was convincing. *América será para Cristo* ("America will belong to Christ") — they sang and everyone believed it was possible.

Missionary leaders from every continent observed the Evangelism-in-Depth movements and began adapting them for application in other parts of the world.

Evangelism in Depth's first national campaign parade in Managua, Nicaragua, 1960

Evangelism in Depth campaign in Maracaibo, Venezuela, 1964 with the participation of the united choir.

Training Pastors in Their Own Villages

In Guatemala the Presbyterians were in trouble with their program of pastoral training. Only a few young men were able to break away from the family farm or business to study in a residence seminary. These were often untried aspirants, frequently tempted to leave their calling and take a job in the city. Those who returned to their villages were out of touch with village life.

Meanwhile, as the mission was training a young man whose future was dubious, a local lay leader was ministering to the people successfully. With ten children and a farm to manage, he could never go to seminary. But he was the obvious leader in that church.

The seminary program was turned upside down, and instead of requiring students to come to the campus, the professors began travelling in a circuit to train those village church lay leaders in their own territory. Thus was born the concept of Theological Education by Extension (TEE).

This, too, attracted the attention of mission leaders everywhere, and extension training of leaders is now, in one form or another, a part of mission strategy everywhere.

Know-how, Government Favors, and Christian Optimism

Technology and science were added to mobilization and training in the missionary's tool kit. There were business planning systems like "PERT"("Program Evaluation and Review Technique"), by which a mission's goals were analyzed and superimposed on a calendar. It was easy to think that once the "PERT chart" was drawn up the job was as good as done. And communications theory seemed to indicate that all one needed to do was to define one's message, select the right medium, and the audience would be convinced. Linguistics and anthropology were added to the repertoire of sciences that assured us that with American know-how, along with the right human and material resources, the song "America will belong to Christ" could come true.

Governments seemed to smile upon evangelical efforts. Special agreements allowed Wycliffe Bible Translators to bring in their airplanes, radio systems and other equipment to work with the Indian tribes.

It did not seem unusual that a chalk-artist evangelist would be invited into a dictator's home to make his presentation.

The post-war years were not seeing great numbers of Latin Americans immediately joining the Gospel People. But foundations were laid. Evangelists multiplied as the Evangelism-in-Depth concept spread the word that every believer is responsible to witness. Pastors' effectiveness improved through TEE types of training programs. Even more important was the confident expectation that the job could be done.

SUGGESTED FURTHER READING:

- William Dayton Roberts *Revolution in Evangelism* (Moody Press of Chicago, 1967). The story of Evangelism-in-Depth in Latin America through its early and "peak" years.

- William Read, Víctor Monterroso, and Harmon Johnson *Latin American Church Growth* (William B. Eerdmanns, 1969). An excellent and comprehensive survey of the Latin American Church up until 1970.

- F. Ross Kinsler. *The Extension Movement in Theological Education* (William Carey Library of Pasadena, 1978, revised edition in 1981). Concepts, history and significance of the movement around the world.

CHAPTER NINE

Ungluing of society

A nine-car, orange-colored train rolls into a Mexico City subway station every two minutes during rush hours. On rubber tires, the train's approach is surprisingly quiet. Thirty-six doors open simultaneously and if the stop is at Pino Suarez or some other major transfer point there is a mad collision of people trying to leave the train and others trying to enter before the buzzer announces that the doors will be shut, ready or not.

"A sauna and a massage" is what some call a ride on the system. The bone-breaking press of bodies provides both the sauna's heat and the massage of physical contact. It can be so intimate that on some lines certain cars are reserved for women and children. Nowhere else

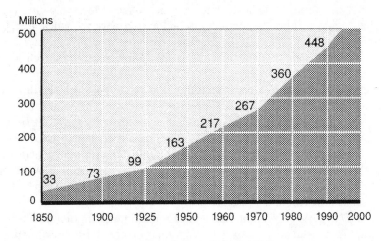

Growth of Latin American Population, 1850—1990

does Latin America's population explosion make such a physical impression.

Families are still large — an average of five in Mexico —but they used to be larger. Families produced many children with the expectation that not all would survive. This is stage I: a high birthrate along with a high death rate, an unhappy but typical equilibrium.

Stage II introduces sanitary health conditions: good water, primary health care, DDT and other benefits. The death rate drops, but mothers may still have eight or ten children. Many third world countries are still in the explosive second stage.

Stage III is a return to an equilibrium, with low birth rates and low death rates. Birth control and new social patterns have been introduced. Much of Latin America is entering stage III, but there's a catch. So many children have been produced during stage II of several years ago, children who are now of child-bearing age, it will take years for the "momentum" of the stage II years to dissipate. Perhaps nothing illustrates the wrenching adjustments taking place in Latin America more than the population problem.

A List of Frustrated Hopes

Raising health standards It was an undeniably worthy goal. What is more humane or Christian than reducing the number of infant deaths? But because other adjustments were not made at the same time, the horrendous, bloated populations of Latin America's cities are the result.

Mass communications Another undeniable need for developing countries. We will never fully appreciate what the transistor radio meant in countries where electricity is slow in reaching the villages. An essay in TIME, "The Transistor Age", described the farmer behind the plow, listening to the transistor radio attached to the horns of his ox. News, entertainment, education are good. But we did not anticipate the rising expectations that radio and television generated. A TV viewer in a cardboard shack sees *Dallas* and becomes aware of consumer goods he will never enjoy in his lifetime. These can be the seeds of revolution.

The green revolution The application of modern agricultural techniques to feed an increasing population is essential. But how frustrating when so much depends on imported petrochemical fertilizers.

Land for the Homesteaders As roads penetrated Amazonia and other unpopulated areas making new lands available for hopeful homesteaders, vast areas suddenly became deforested. Jungle soils yielded excellent harvests for a few years but did not have sufficient minerals for year-after-year harvesting. Farmers who "slash and burn" the forest to carve out a farm then abandon the land to erosion, move on to slash and burn again.

Agricultural exports A century ago don Pedro, the wealthy land-owner, raised only food for local consumption with the help of the sharecroppers on his land. His *hacienda* (estate) was quite isolated and there was no international market for his product. Now better roads and an international market for some other kind of crop — cotton or beef perhaps — mean more cash for Don Pedro's heirs who manage the farm. But the country ends up importing expensive food. And less labor-intensive crops mean that the poor sharecroppers are laid off and join the millions seeking a place to live in the capital.

Industrialization An international company sets up a factory, but then a neighboring country (whose workers may be less organized and whose demands are more modest) attracts the industry. The company, often with callous disregard for the thousands it may leave unemployed, moves to where production is cheaper. Such "transnational" firms are not viewed with much affection in Latin America.

Loans for development Like newlyweds besieged by salesmen offering them house appliances on credit, Latin American countries have been encouraged to borrow. If the young husband loses his job and he can't make the payments, the refrigerator can be repossessed. When oil prices drop and Venezuela can't make the payments, how-ever, you can't repossess a subway system. Unpaid debts grow bigger with the interest charges.

Stability (Often military aid is seen as a source of stability "so that a country can concentrate on development.") Guns, however, often get into the hands of the local establishment that is interested only in holding on to power. Desperate people call for a change. Of course, the communists are there to take advantage of the situation about to explode. "Stability" often ends up with soldiers in battle dress on the street corners, and planes dropping U.S.-made bombs on Indian villages.

Nothing has turned out right.

The Alliance for Progress did not meet its goal of seeing Latin America's economy "take off". The reason for this is perceived by some to be a basic character flaw in Latin America, shaped by its centuries of colonial history. Others propose a "dependency theory", blaming the industrialized nations for creating a system which will always leave the Third World dependent.

Cuba — Communist as of 1960 — provided a "valid" reason for neighbor countries to assume hard-line political control. Military governments became the rule for a period in most of the Latin American nations. Death squads, *los desaparecidos* (people who simply disappeared), bombings of "rebel" Indian villages, closing down of university campuses, became common in many countries.

The military uniforms finally began to disappear from presidential palaces in the 1980s, as some of the major countries returned to democratic rule — Argentina, Chile, and Brazil, among others. But the spectacular post-World War II growth, with its stunning hotels, jet-age airports, highways, dams, and handsome university campuses, had already begun to slow down. In the 1980s, economic growth in many countries was *negative*. This is a way of saying things were going backwards.

The 1980s ("The Lost Decade" according to Latin American economists) was a period of recession as severe as the U.S. depression of the 1930s. Hoping for relief, Third World people vainly watched the news about the periodic meetings of the heads of the industrialized nations. Most of the time no pronouncement was made regarding anything that might heal the wounds of the South. The cards seemed stacked in favor of the already industrialized nations. They set the prices of the coffee bought in Latin America and the tractors they sold in return.

But much of the blame lies in Latin America too. Venezuelan Christian leaders, for example, see no need for their country to be poor, given its mineral resources, the high level of education of its people, and the fact that Venezuelans themselves are in control of their oil production — not foreigners. They point to corruption at every level of society as the cause. Likewise, in other countries, Latin American presidents were known to siphon off billions (not millions) of dollars, for themselves.

"The Gospel Is Preached to the Poor"

In the midst of the poverty and the frustration caused by greed both in their own countries as well as in the North, the Gospel People have been growing in number.

Critics look at them and say that evangelicals meeting to praise God and sing choruses in the present situation is cowardly escapism. The Pentecostal churches in Chile are a "refuge" of the "masses", according to one sociologist. Other social scientists call the phenomenon a symbolic rebellion against the status quo. Others see in the evangelical movement a device of the capitalist nations, even of the CIA, to keep Latin Americans content with their lot, a movement to deter communist takeovers.

One critic has had to admit, however, that money flowing from the U.S. can never account for the spontaneous growth of the evangelical church now going on. It is no artificial structure propped up by foreign funds.

To simply state that evangelical churches multiply most where there is poverty, insecurity and violence leads us into a trap. "So you are for poverty so that your churches can grow?" critics seem to say.

To agree that evangelical preachers point to Christ's second coming as the only final solution to the human problem is only to hear the critics say "There now, we knew you weren't interested in our present condition."

There are churches and missionaries that seem blind to the grinding poverty about them — but not all.

The missionary movement in Latin America faces a conspiracy of slander which denies the fact that a Christian can rejoice when the "Gospel is preached to the poor," while at the same time deploring poverty; that a Christian can anticipate Christ's glorious kingdom while working to relieve suffering here; that Christian missionaries have sincere theological motives to reach people for Christ instead of, allegedly, acting as spies for the CIA.

A map of the distribution of Mexico City's evangelical churches reveals scores of congregations in the poverty-stricken Nezahualcoyotl area (and few evangelical churches in the fancy suburbs to the west). In their desperation, the poor are eager to receive the gospel.

Helping Your Neighbor Quietly

It is true that many evangelical churches consider participation in the local community associations, political parties or even in the local soccer team as "worldly." So they are branded unconcerned about the needs of people around them, "on strike" as far as helping to improve conditions in the present world.

But let us not judge evangelical believers too harshly. They have

The dwellings of the poor in the favelas *of Sao Paulo, Brazil*

Squatters' reed huts in the pueblos jóvenes *of Lima, Peru*

seen treasurers take off with a cooperative's funds, and they have been "burned" by too many politicians' promises. Without fanfare they may help a neighbor pay his light bill or get a job for a new Christian. The pastor may not preach about social reform; this could even be considered subversive in some countries. But the primitive instincts of new Christians lead them to help.

A woman psychologist assigned to work with delinquents in Venezuela's reformatories became convinced that the only real solution was to take in the street children before they became part of the gangs. As a Christian she founded a network of homes where substitute parents receive the children and raise them in a Christian atmosphere. Volunteers from evangelical churches come in regularly and do the washing or teach classes in certain subjects. This is no top-heavy institution funded with foreign mission money but the spontaneous love of Venezuelan Christians in action.

Four-fifths of all Latin Americans are poor. The Gospel People are growing in a world that has come unglued. In their poverty they find hope in Christ. They are growing, too, because people who are needy often see in their Christian neighbors a love and concern about their situation.

SUGGESTED FURTHER READING:

- Thomas E. Skidmore and Peter H. Smith *Modern Latin America* (Oxford University Press of Cambridge, 1989). A good study of the economic and social condition of the region today.

- Peter Worsley *The Three Worlds: Culture and World Development* (University of Chicago Press, 1964).

- Eduardo Galeano *Open Veins of Latin America* (Monthly Review Press of New York, 1973). This classic work represents much of the literature regarding Latin America in which the region's problems are attributed to U.S. foreign policy and the practices of transnational companies.

CHAPTER TEN

Cities — concentrated chaos

Carmen has lived in an adobe hut, hard by a filthy stream on the edge of a Latin American capital, for most of her adult life. Attracted by the city's bright lights, her family migrated to the city when she was but a teenager from a small village far away in the green mountains.

Today, Carmen is the mother of nine children, almost all with different fathers. She and the children often forage in the nearby garbage dump as a means of putting food on the table. Each day is a fearful grind of misery. But as the children grow, she at least keeps the family together with the help of her mate, Ramón, father of her youngest child.

Carmen and her neighbors generally live on the edge of town. They are the abysmally poor of the infamous squatter villages (*barrios* in some countries, *tugurios*, *favelas*, or *pueblos jóvenes* in others), the growing slums that ring the cities or are lumped together in ugly welts throughout the urban sprawl. Unlike the poor in North America's inner-cities, Latin America's desperately poor usually live far from the downtown area.

For one-half of Latin America's city people it is an impossible day-to-day existence. Read Oscar Lewis's *Five Families* and feel the force of the concern repeated so often in one form or another: "Where is our next meal coming from?"

By the time you arrive at Carmen's house, the street has dwindled away. It's the end of the line, a dusty path that fails to appear on any city map.

Carmen and Ramón and the nine children live in two rooms, one of which is a kitchen. Water comes from an outside spigot serving a dozen homes. They have electricity, stolen from nearby cables by a makeshift connection in a spiderweb tangle of wires, to power the lights and television set. There is no thought of a telephone and a closet serves as a commode with a nearby trench for waste water.

Twelve hours a night Ramón drives a cab. At the end of his stint Alejandro, his relief driver, takes over the ancient VW beetle and pushes it through daytime traffic for another twelve. The vehicle's owner holds them responsible for dents and collects a fixed "rent" whether the amount has been collected in fares or not.

Carmen and Ramón, like thousands of other squatters, are sometimes called *paracaidistas* ("parachuters") or *invasores* ("invaders"). They, with a group of several hundred families, may descend upon some unused land overnight, setting up shacks of plastic sheeting, corrugated iron, flattened out oil drums or scrap lumber.

It's bad press for the government to send in the police or the army to dislodge them, but this is often done. In some places if a family can prove it has lived continuously on the land for a year, the ground can become theirs. This becomes a cat-and-mouse game as squatters somehow elude the police but never leave the property.

Eventually the government may buy the land from its owner and with the cooperation of the squatters' committee, lay out orderly streets. But it may take years for the barrio to get legitimate electricity, running water or pavement for its muddy streets, a sewage system, or regular bus service. Once the squatters have some assurance that they will not be evicted, concrete block gradually begins to replace the corrugated iron siding, window frames are added. Across the years the block gets plastered and the plaster gets painted. Reinforcing rods may stick out of the roof pointing to the sky — signs of hope that perhaps a second floor may yet be added.

In some cities tourists are spared the sight of these squatter settlements. In Lima the slums are visible, stretching miles across the desert between the airport and the city. In other cities they scar the sides of the mountains, replacing the forested slopes with huts that seem to be piled one on top of the other.

Not a Global Village—But a Global City

The social chaos in Latin America cannot be understood without giving special attention to the cities where this chaos is concentrated.

The major social fact of the 20th century is the huge increase of city

Play in the mean streets of Sao Paulo

people in the world. Urbanization is the process whereby the proportion of city inhabitants increases at the expense of rural populations. But more than that, the "way of the city" — its style, its language, its music, its values — increasingly dominates the rest of the country. At least 400 cities in the world have at least a million inhabitants. In the next 7 seconds 31 babies will be born, half of them in cities. In Latin America the number of people living in cities increased from 48.8% to 57.7% between 1960 and 1980. By 2000, there will be 548 million Latin Americans of which 67.7% will be city people.

Certain countries (including the U.S.) will be almost totally urban by 2000. Only Guatemala, Ecuador, and Paraguay will have more rural people than urban, mainly because these countries have large Indian populations. *(See the chart on the next page.)*

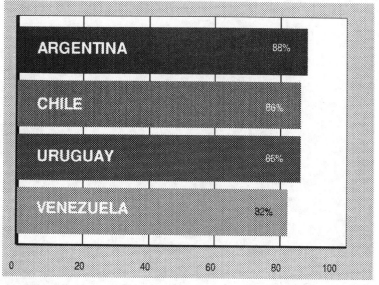

Percentage of Population in Urban Areas, Year 2000 — Selected Countries

The City as Parasite

Both a push and a pull makes Latin America's cities grow.

The *push* comes from the general population increase. Added to that is a surplus of rural people driven to the city as traditional crops are supplanted by less labor-intensive produce. It takes fewer workers to raise beef for McDonald's hamburgers than to raise strawberries or coffee.

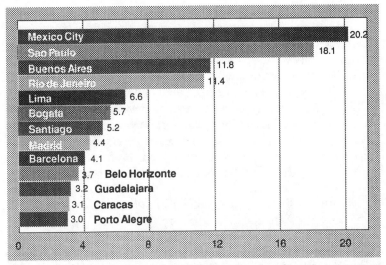

Population of Cities in Spanish and Portuguese-speaking Countries

In some countries, guerrillas extort money and food from rural peasants. Then, the army often threatens them if they don't reveal which way the guerrillas went. Caught in the cross-fire, the farmers move out.

New roads carrying hopeful homesteaders to the slash-and-burn farms also make it easier for the discouraged peasant to flee to the city.

The *pull* is the hope for jobs, better schools, hospitals, and other social services in the city.

Because political power resides in the cities, tax money is generally spent for the city's handsome university library or the extravagant monument to the nation's heroes instead of for desks in country schools. Cities absorb most of the resources of the nation.

An example of this process is vividly portrayed in Mexico City. One out of four Mexicans live here. The capital grows by a million people a year — about 600,000 by birth and 400,000 by migration. A million new jobs have to be created each year to meet the expectations of those entering the job market.

The average age of Mexico's City's population is 14.2 (In Chicago, the average age is 31.). This means there are 9 or 10 million children — more than the population of New York City.

Due to its altitude (7200 feet), the city's air is composed of only one-half of the oxygen found in cities at sea level. Almost surrounding the city rise the mountains that prevent vapors from escaping the basin. Two majestic volcanoes, side by side, used to dominate the skyline, but they are seldom visible now. The lead, carbon monoxide and other air pollutants are poisoning the inhabitants. At times birds fall out of the sky, killed by some cloud of noxious fumes.

The city is a gigantic parasite, devouring water, material resources and some of the most ambitious and aggressive people from the entire nation. At each cardinal point of the city an enormous bus station receives the *campesinos*, who unload their pitiful cardboard boxes tied by string and their bundles of clothes. Over a thousand new people arrive each day.

We ask: "Isn't there some natural limit to the number of people who can crowd into a limited urban area?"

In some cities, the squatter settlements seek for space by creeping up the sides of the surrounding mountains. As the settlements reach upward, the slopes become steeper, and the precarious homesites are often washed away by land slides.

Mexico City has space for urban sprawl, but water is running short. Originally the city was built on a lake, so there is ground water. But wells drawing the water from the soil cause the ground to settle. Buildings sink and tilt at surprising angles. So, wells are now illegal, but a major new and more adequate water system is economically unfeasible.

Street Corner Tortillas

Late-rising Mexicans on their way to work swallow a tortilla and something to drink bought from the street vendor. Contraband transistor radios and stolen music cassettes in makeshift stands on the subway entrance steps complicate a commuter's descent into the station. In cities where authorities are less tolerant, a signalman is posted. His warning that the police are coming causes a magical and sudden disappearance of all the vendors on the block.

A serious study done by a Peruvian economist revealed how much of Lima's business takes place in what is known as the "informal sector." In addition to business on the streets, furniture gets repaired, clothing manufactured and cars overhauled in people's homes and back yards. He documented how difficult it is to secure a license to establish a business because of government bureaucracy, even if someone wanted to operate legally.

This trade does not get registered in the country's economic statistics. It pays no taxes to governments strapped for cash. And millions of citizens in the informal sector are outside government health programs and have no provision for their old age.

Unemployment in Latin America's cities has forced people to scramble for a living. The wholesaler who distributes the products for sale in the street may even get rich in the informal sector. But for the poorest, there is only slightly more dignity in hawking brooms than in begging.

"Wash your car, mister?"

You see them — the street children — everywhere in Latin America's sprawling cities. They are the victims of economic depression and political violence — abandoned and runaway, missing and unwanted, abused and starving.

An estimated 2 million live in the streets of Mexico City. In Brazil a conservative estimate has 9.5 million children living in the streets and 2 million girls between the ages of 9 and 13 working as prostitutes.

Many times the child is an unexpected or unwanted accident in the life of a poor family. Such children are burdens to their parents, who simply wait for them to reach the age of 8 or 9, when they can be more self-sufficient as well as help their younger brothers and sisters. Until then, they are considered unproductive, especially if the child is a girl. In effect, a childhood does not exist for these children.

Violence in the cities, whether through terrorism or by other causes, produces many orphans. Tragically, some children actually witness the murder or death of their parents.

With people becoming poorer, they simply cannot provide for the children of their families. And so, thousands of the kids are abandoned — expelled outright — or turned out into the streets to help the family by earning income. Later some discover they would rather stay in the streets than return home.

Those who have no home live in the side-streets and alleyways, sleep crowded together on hot-air vents in sidewalks, root through garbage and survive in gangs — like packs of animals, blending into

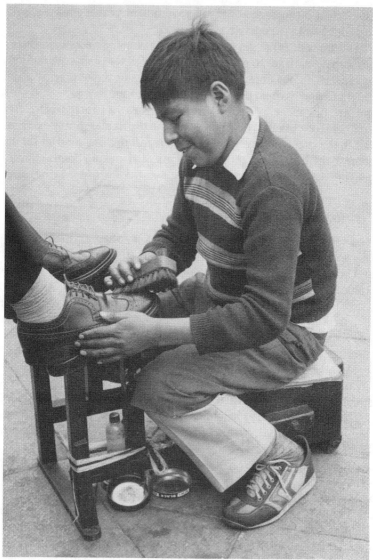

"I shine your shoes, mister"

the scenery.

The street kids fall victim to the drug traffickers and other crimi-
nals simply because they are a public nuisance — like stray dogs. In

Thousands of children live and sleep on the sidewalks and streets of Latin America.

some countries they are being massacred by death squads or vigilantes — hundreds annually in Brazil.

Millions of children wash cars, guard them, too, when the owners are away, carry bags for people, shine shoes, sell candy, steal, and often die in the mean streets of Latin America's cities.

Where Are the Gospel People?

It is sad to note that most of the tremendous growth of the evangelical church in Latin America has been in rural areas, the *pueblos*, towns and smaller cities of the region. With the exception of Central America's cities and Santiago, Chile, there has been proportionately little church growth in the larger cities until recently.

Of the total population there is no more than 3% Protestant in such

The garbage foragers — a common sight in Latin American cities

mega-cities as Buenos Aires, Sao Paulo, Río de Janeiro, Lima, Bogotá, Caracas, Medellín, and Mexico City. In Mexico City a 1986 survey discovered only 240,000 in the Protestant community out of a population of over 20 million. In Lima a 1986 survey revealed only 1.8% were Protestants. As impressive as are some of the big churches in these cities, they still reach only a small proportion of the people.

Pastors and churches, with notable exceptions, tend to be overwhelmed by the city's masses of humanity, the secular spirit and its complexity. Traditionally, the evangelistic orientation of the church has been rural.

Not all people of the city are as poor as Carmen. Even in the worst of the slums, people are not walking about with fists held upward in anger against the system, (as the communist literature might lead us to believe). Life goes on, with its weddings, fiestas and funerals.

And so the church, too, moves on. It may meet in an unfinished shell of a building or in a former automobile showroom, refurbished by willing volunteers, without money for Sunday School materials. It may be directed by a pastor with at best an evening Bible school education, himself a mechanic. Struggling against impossible odds, God's people meet, pray, sing, worship, hear God's Word, and win others.

SUGGESTED FURTHER READING:

- Raymond J. Bakke *The Urban Christian* (InterVarsity Press of Downers Grove, IL, 1987). A description of the author's pastoral work in a multi-ethnic Chicago community with suggestions as to its application to urban areas in other parts of the world.

- Alma Guillermoprieto "Letter from Medellín," *The New Yorker* (April 22, 1991; Pp. 96-108). A graphic presentation of life among young people in the drug-infested *barrios* of Medellín.

- Oscar Lewis *Five Families: Mexican Case Studies in the Culture of Poverty* (Basic of New York, 1959). This classic work describes in real-life situations the hopeless existence of the urban poor.

- John Maust *Cities of Change. Urban Growth and God's People in Ten Latin American Cities* (Latin America Mission, Miami, FL., 1984). A well-described work with an across-the-board look at what evangelicals are doing. Well-illustrated.

- Roger Greenway *An Urban Strategy for Latin America* (Baker Book House of Grand Rapids, 1973). This urban missiologist suggests strategies for urban ministry, drawing from his experience in Mexico City.

- Robert Linthicum *City of God, City of Satan* (Zondervan Publishers of Grand Rapids, 1991). A comprehensive Biblical theology of the urban church. Former urban pastor and community worker, the author is director of World Vision's Urban Advance.

The challenge
of Latin
America's cities

CHAPTER ELEVEN

Cracks in the monolith

Camilo Torres was gunned down by the Colombian army in the rugged mountains of his country on February 15, 1967, at the age of 38. Although he died a guerrilla, he had been a priest, a symbol of a church divided, part of it turning revolutionary. ¡*Torres vive!* ("Torres still lives!") continues to be scrawled on many an adobe wall.

Son of a physician in Bogotá, after seminary he studied sociology in Europe. While serving as a chaplain in a Colombian university he became actively involved in development projects for the poor.

Torres's compassion for the poor and his frustration with the usual process of development led him to the conviction that the only effective change in the situation would be for the masses to take power. He felt Christians were obliged to topple established economic and social structures for the benefit of the vast majority of the people. Armed struggle was the only answer. A year before his death he proclaimed, "Liberation or death!"

Accused by some of being a communist, his clear statements said otherwise. He also denied being an anti-communist and said he was even willing to fight beside communists with a common purpose of pulling down the ruling class, breaking the yoke of U.S. control in Latin America and empowering the masses. Torres hoped to install national socialism without destroying his basic Christianity. His would be a stance between the Soviet block on the one hand and the West on the other.

The Roman Church did not approve of his views nor of his taking up arms, but Torres never gave up his Catholic faith — not even at the end.

Camilo Torres's pilgrimage and death inspired many Latin American Catholics to carry their commitment to social justice to its ultimate consequences.

Updating the Musty Structures

Ascending the papal throne in 1958, an unlikely 77-year-old pope, John XXIII, set the wheels in motion that led to widespread change, including revolutionary Catholicism in Latin America. His concern was that the church had not kept up with the accelerated social change since the end of the Second World War, a dozen years earlier. He felt that an *aggiornamento* (roughly, "an updating") was necessary if the church were to speak meaningfully to the modern world in the last half of the 20th century.

To this end, the Second Vatican Council was called by Pope John and took place in Rome 1962 to 1965. Unprecedented broad representation of the church, including great numbers from the Third World, met as "shepherds of the Catholic fold" to respond to the issues of a society in a state of rapid change and transformation.

The council decreed that the mass would now be heard in the languages of the people; the priest would face the congregation; new encouragement would be given to reading the Bible. Vatican II also opened the doors of the church to a "broader kind of fellowship" — an openness not only to non-Catholic Christians but to all of humanity.

Many Protestant missionaries arriving in Latin America in the fifties had found themselves outcasts in a society dominated by the Catholic hierarchy. In just a few years in some places they were being accepted as "separated brethren" and some were even involved in regular prayer sessions with priests.

But most important, Pope John's efforts — plus those of Pope Paul VI beginning in 1963 — and the documents of the Second Vatican Council greatly encouraged those Catholics hoping for a kind of renewal that would meet the overwhelming needs of the poor and the oppressed.

Going Further Than Expected

Broad social involvement in the Roman Catholic Church can be viewed through the lens of the Latin American Episcopal Council

A militant revolutionary expresses his profound belief in Christ.

(CELAM) and its first three bishops' conferences.

The first one, convened by Pope Pius XII in Río de Janeiro, Brazil, in 1955, focused on typical issues of that period, such as the "Protestant danger," the peril of Communism, and the need for new Catholic missionaries to Latin America. There was a certain fortress mentality and a preoccupation with clerical problems.

Lots of water had passed under the bridge with the Vatican Council and its aftermath when the Latin American bishops' second conference was convened in Medellín, Colombia, that most Catholic of all cities. It was 1968.

Observers were surprised to hear Sergio Méndez, Bishop of Cuernavaca, Mexico, say: "Capitalism cannot fulfill the Christian promise of well-being for the common man. The only road for the development of Latin America is socialism."

The Medellín conference demonstrated a certain courage to turn and face toward the impoverished masses — to recognize Latin American realities and to seek to place Catholic "presence" among the poor. This watershed conference:

- Criticized both Capitalist and Marxist systems for violating human dignity,
- Rejected violence under most circumstances, opposed violators of human rights, especially the then-current dictatorships,
- Encouraged Latin American unity and regional nationalism,
- Urged a democratization of education, recommending Paulo Freire's educational methods. Freire, a Brazilian, felt that education should include the development of a social conscience and an awareness of the unequal distribution of wealth and power,
- Identified peace with justice — without a just economic system, Latin America would never enjoy peace.

An anti-communist line was hardly heard. Much attention was paid to the burden of capitalism — the flight of capital, unpayable foreign loans, and the need for greater economic independence. "Our countries are not the owners of productivity nor do they make the financial decisions. This has inevitable consequences."

One wonders how it was that these bishops, most of them extremely conservative, signed such a document. Obviously, the progressives came to Medellín prepared — the conservatives were unprepared. But this is not the end of the tale.

Facing 1979 Realities in Puebla

Eleven years later (1979) in historic Puebla, Mexico, CELAM called the third general bishops' conference. By then the panorama had changed noticeably. The heady revolutionary atmosphere of Medellín had collided with real-life, totalitarian, right-wing, military regimes in such countries as Chile, Argentina, Brazil and Guatemala. Even the expression coined in Medellín, "the Church's option for the poor," was being interpreted as subversive.

To evangelicals used to hearing about Catholic persecution of Protestants, it was a switch to hear about Catholic martyrs. A report presented at Puebla listed a total of 1500 priests, bishops, nuns, and active lay persons who had been arrested, tortured, kidnapped, assassinated, or exiled between 1968 and 1978.

Meanwhile, John Paul II had become pope. A Pole who had suffered under a Marxist regime, he was critical of materialistic dialectic ideology. And by now the conservatives had won a controlling hand in CELAM.

The discussion soon polarized around the theme of Catholic social and political action. The results were generally a step back from the more radical positions of Medellín and included criticism of Marxism. But they did not turn back from their commitment to the poor.

But the Tiger Is Loose

Between the Medellín and Puebla conferences "Liberation Theology" or "Theologies" had spread to many sectors of the Roman Church in Latin America.

Its birth date is often assigned to the 1968 Medellín conference, but there was a long period of gestation before that time. European thought had also been influencing Latin American theologians.

In the early 1960s Gustavo Gutiérrez, a Peruvian priest, began asking how the church could establish a dialogue with its Latin American constituents. He proposed a new focus that would respond to the people's needs. He met with theologians from Uruguay and Argentina in Brazil, and just before the Medellín conference gave a lecture in Chimbote, Peru, entitled "Toward a Theology of Liberation."

The year of the Medellín conference, Pope Paul VI visited Colombia, the first trip ever to Latin America by a pope. Three thousand priests gave him a tumultuous welcome in Bogotá. He spoke about "bonds of love" at an international eucharistic congress. He met with the poor. He quoted his encyclical (a papal letter to the church's bishops), *Populorum Progressio*, calling for a more equal distribution of wealth and land. He stressed peaceful, gradual reform.

But the specter of Camilo Torres, slain a short while before, haunted the atmosphere. Brazil's Archbishop Helder Camara described the setting as a "pre-revolutionary climate." He added that he hoped for peace, but also respected those who were led in good conscience to take the option for revolution.

Shortly after Medellín in 1971, Gutiérrez's book, *A Theology of Liberation*, was published — a study recognized as the original, guiding work of the movement. However, neither Gutiérrez nor any other author is considered to have the last word on the subject. Rather than a sharply defined theological system, it is a product of a group of theologians, many with contradictory opinions, whose stream of thought is still flowing and evolving.

Doing Theology Among the Poor

1. Liberation Theology *starts with the situation* — an in-depth study of Latin America's social problems. It makes its contribution to theology by utilizing the social sciences. This is in marked contrast with theology of the North (or the West) which "has its being" in a philosophical frame of reference. Traditional theology has been written to answer the questions philosophers often raise. L.T. has made theologians realize more clearly how much traditional doctrinal systems had been influenced by Greek philosophy.

This basic posture leads liberation thinking to an interpretation of the Scriptures almost entirely controlled by the immediate situation in which the theologian is living.

2. In the liberationist's approach, *social analysis* is important. How does one explain "the way things are?" Marx provides tools of analysis which liberation theologians indicate work well in the Latin American situation. Using such tools to read the Bible leads to one-sided interpretations and selectivity in emphasizing certain passages. For the redemptive conflict with Satan, sin, and death — the heart of the gospel — it largely substitutes struggle between classes. It has also

tended to reshape the Savior and Lord of Scriptural revelation into a mere sociopolitical Liberator.

3. *"A new way of doing theology"* is the liberationist's expression indicating that the Theology of Liberation is not a new theme for discussion, but rather, a wholly new approach. It means thinking critically about *praxis* — which is one's actions in response to the social and political situation — in Latin America, in this case, only after becoming involved and doing something about it is anyone capable then of "doing theology." This is in contrast to the traditional approach of the North which begins by thinking, and then acting upon what one has thought about.

4. A guiding principle of early Liberation Theology was that underdevelopment in the Third World is the result of economic *dependence* of the poor countries upon the rich nations. Old 19th century colonialism has been replaced by a "neo-colonialism." Third World poverty, they contend, is the underside of the First World's wealth, providing its raw material and cheap labor.

This approach comes out of L.T.'s serious confrontation with oppression in society and its emphasis on an option for the poor.

Running Away from Politics

As of the 1970s when Liberation Theology began being preached from many a Catholic pulpit, the Gospel People began to find more disenchanted Roman Catholics inquiring at their doors, for good reasons and bad. There were good reasons in that some, sensing that with the call for revolutionary action by the priests, spiritual needs were not being met — needs they found fulfilled as they found Christ in evangelical churches.

But there were bad reasons as well, in that these were often middle-class Latin Americans who wanted to escape grappling with the tough issue of what a Christian's responsibility is towards the poor. They themselves were holding on tightly to what they had.

After the Medellín conference, the severe cracks in the monolithic Roman Catholic Church in Latin America were clear for all to see.

SUGGESTED FURTHER READING:

- Gustavo Gutiérrez *A Theology of Liberation* (Orbis Books of Maryknoll, New York, 1973). The classic exposition of liberation theology by its "father."

- Phillip Berryman *Liberation Theology* (Temple University Press of Philadelphia, 1987). Concise, helpful guide to "essential facts about the revolutionary movement in Latin America and beyond" by a pastoral worker in Panama and later with the American Friends Service Committee in Central America.

- Emilio Nuñez *Liberation Theology* (Moody Press of Chicago, 1985). A Latin American evangelical's response to liberation theology.

CHAPTER TWELVE

The cracks widen

While celebrating mass in March of 1980, in San Salvador, Archbishop Oscar Romero was assassinated. He was the highest Roman Catholic cleric of the country, a conservative and scholarly type. His death represents serious escalation of violence since Torres took up arms in Colombia.

The downtown Catholic cathedral, destroyed by fire several years previously, had been under reconstruction. But Romero had suspended the work so the Church's limited resources could be used for direct pastoral work among the poor.

For those accustomed to a centuries-old Catholicism with its golden altars, incense-filled ceremony and somber priests in brocaded robes, this was a radical change. Romero had taken seriously the Biblical texts such as Amos 5:21-25 and Hosea 6:6 — "For it is steadfast love that I desire, not sacrifice, and acknowledgement of God rather than burnt sacrifices."

Romero's steadfast love for the poor led to several consequences. According to Jon Sobrino, a priest in the same country, it led to Romero's denunciation of the idolatry of money, military and political power, corruption, falsehood, and U.S. imperialism. It led to his affirming the right of peasants to join militant people's organizations. At the same time he cautioned them not to let their faith be absorbed completely by politics. And it led to his death.

A New Church vs. a New Military

The Roman Catholic Church had always exercised tremendous political and economic influence in Latin American society. The *Opus Dei* organization encouraged Catholics to occupy key positions in every country. Certain political parties and trade unions had always been under strong Church influence. However, since Vatican II and the Medellín and Puebla conferences a whole new self-understanding developed. More of the Church's objectives would be accomplished outside its walls. And its purposes were not tied to its self-interest, but to the needs of the poor.

As this was happening, a new role for the military in Latin America began developing. The region had a long history of *caudillos*. There were the traditional dictators — Perón in Argentina, Strossener in Paraguay, Vargas in Brazil, Jiménez in Venezuela, and the Somozas in Nicaragua. But in the middle of the last half of the 20th century the military *as an institution* took over one country after another until more than half the nations were ruled with an iron hand.

A large newly militant section of the Church found itself at loggerheads with these new military governments. Sometimes the military, trying to seek more popular support, courted the Protestants. General Pinochet and his staff made appearances at the large Methodist Pentecostal Cathedral in Santiago, Chile, as did General Gaerastazú Médici at a large Baptist church in Sao Paulo, Brazil.

The situation became more complicated in Cuba under Castro and in Nicaragua under the Sandinistas. Latin America will not soon forget the TV images of a conservative Pope John Paul II angrily crying "silencio" while being shouted down by the pro-Sandinista Catholics of the "Church of the People." The official Church of Nicaragua was critical of the government but a large sector of Nicaraguan Catholics were pro-Sandinista.

The cracks had widened and the Latin American Catholic Church would never be the same again.

Less Tension — At Least for Now

In the 1980s one country after another returned to democratic rule. By 1990, Cuba remained the only Latin republic whose chief of state wore a military uniform.

At the same time serious thinkers in the Liberation Theology stream began to widen their concerns. There is now a marked and needed emphasis in their recent literature about spirituality. Standing with the poor and freedom from oppression is still central, but more is being said about the unity of history, salvation, the nature and work of Christ, and the church.

Liberation Theology has changed the face of Latin American revolution. The Sandinista regime in Nicaragua was no longer just another case of "godless, atheistic communism." Billboards declared *Entre religión y revolución: no hay contradicción* ("Between Religion and Revolution: there is no contradiction"). Even Fidel Castro, hardly concerned about the spiritual aspects of Christianity, made what many saw as a surprising about-face and in his interviews with Brazilian priest Frei Betto defended the kind of Christianity that would support a revolution (*Fidel y la religión* — "Fidel and Religion," 1985).

And the Gospel People?

As early as 1960 a Protestant organization ISAL ("Church and Society in Latin America") was founded in Argentina with the participation of several radical Roman Catholic theologians. ISAL was a forum for liberals to study all of the options for radically changing society. It became one of the bridges over which Roman Catholic Liberation Theology and Protestant liberal theology arrived in Latin America.

Not that Liberation Theology is just another form of classical Protestant liberalism. U.S. evangelicals used to sort out the liberals by asking them questions about the inspiration of Scriptures and the deity of Jesus Christ. But applying the usual statement of faith to see if a Latin American theologian will sign it just does not work. He or she may not have any problem with the Scriptures or the person of Christ. The issue now is his or her agenda — what they consider to be the primary mission of the church.

Some Latin American Protestants have bought into Liberation Theology. Many of those who have, though by no means all, are from the least Latin American of the denominations — churches that are related closely to North American and European main-line denominations.

Most of the more grass-roots Latin American churches will have nothing to do with this "Latin American theology." Because they themselves have come out of Roman Catholicism, most evangelicals will almost automatically reject anything that emerges from the Roman Church. Applying Romans 13 unconditionally, they cannot join a revolution. They distrust anything that looks like Marxism. And, most of all, Liberation Theology does not say much about what is most precious to them — their personal conversion experience.

Having done little formal theological thinking about the Christian's responsibility to the poor — most of them *are* the poor — and being unprepared to discuss the issue, they often reject anybody and anything that has to do with Liberation Theology.

Denominations and churches have suffered painful splits as the Latin American Protestant movement has become polarized. Those sympathetic to issues of liberation, justice and concern for society are almost completely isolated from those whose prime concern is evangelism and the growth of the church.

Some in the middle — and getting shot at from both sides — are trying to hold on to both concerns.

Not All Is Revolution

Despite the splash of attention that Liberation Theology has attracted

A Roman Catholic charismatic middle-class group meets in a home.

in the First World, other quieter changes are taking place among Latin American Catholics.

Many evangelical bookstore managers have found that more Bibles and Christian books are sold to Roman Catholics than to evangelicals. There is an amazing openness to possess and read the Bible. Many priests and bishops encourage the people to buy it, even in Protestant versions.

Perhaps the greatest change in Latin American Catholicism is the participation of laymen and laywomen. With the shortage of priests, ordinary Catholics are being trained and sent out as *Delegados de la Palabra* ("Delegates of the Word") to conduct Bible studies. Others perform additional ministries formerly carried out only by priests. Nuns with simple skirts and blouses are another evidence of change.

Watching some religious TV program with its use of popular tunes (sometimes borrowed evangelical choruses) with guitar accompaniment, and testimonies of lay people, a viewer may have to wait a long time for some clue that in fact the program is Catholic.

Cursillos to bring together leaders for training, fellowship, or marriage enrichment; healing campaigns; attractive Bible study materials — all point to a Church that is in renewal — but within Roman Catholic parameters.

Multiplying Cell Groups

Latin American Catholics also have discovered the small group. The observance of the mass in a cavernous cathedral does not meet the needs of participatory Bible study and prayer, and the sharing of one's concerns. Meeting this need is the multiplication of "grass-roots church communities." These *Comunidades eclesiales de base* (CEBs) are also usually led by lay people.

But this is no typical InterVarsity Bible study in a dorm. CEBs are more likely to be a group of Catholic factory workers reading the Bible in a shanty town on the edge of an industrial city in Brazil. And their concerns are not just personal spiritual enrichment, but *concientización* (creating a social conscience), and then seeing what action may be taken to correct a social problem in their community. Should a protest be launched to demand better drinking water or should a health clinic be established for the neighborhood?

The *cursillo* movement focuses on marital problems, alcoholism, and other individual dilemmas. But the CEBs for the most part share the concerns of Liberation Theology.

In Brazil alone at its peak, there were an estimated 70,000 to 80,000 CEBs with perhaps a total of 2.5 million participants. In a monumental study about Brazilian CEBs (*The Expectation of the Poor*), Guillermo Cook noted that they were "challenging the traditional Catholic pyramidal church structure," an "example of a grassroots revolt against institutional fossilization." Bishops wondered how to control a movement which grants status to everyone who participates. Such lay people are making all kinds of new demands on the Church.

There is some evidence to show that the Church is applying restrictions on the CEBs. Many of the participants are moving into the Pentecostal fold.

Another Kind of Liberation

A missionary in Colombia announced a lecture on Liberation Theology. To his surprise many Catholic charismatics showed up. After hearing about Christian responsibility in an oppressive society, the charismatics complained: "But he didn't say anything about liberation!" To them, liberation was deliverance from demonic powers, the exorcism of individuals.

The Catholic charismatic movement opened another crack in the ancient Church. Catholic Father Francis McNutt from the U.S. and Pentecostal David du Plessis from Africa fanned the flames of a sudden awareness of the power and gifts of the Holy Spirit among Latin American Catholics. The early 1970s witnessed the multiplication of charismatic prayer groups in homes, churches where participants clapped and danced; healing campaigns and seminars were scheduled on "How to Receive the Holy Spirit." This was liberation in another dimension, and it coincided with a charismatic renewal in many of the traditional non-Pentecostal evangelical churches as well.

In some countries evangelicals mixed freely with the renewed Catholics in their Bible studies. But Pope John Paul II initiated a subtle move to control the Catholic charismatics. First, the World Catholic Charismatic headquarters were moved from Belgium to the Vatican. Second, a "shepherd" coordinator was appointed for each country to direct the local movement.

Many such Catholics, having tasted now of a personal relationship with Christ and having discovered the Bible for themselves, individually abandoned the Church to join evangelical groups. Some entire charismatic communities also left the Roman fold, eventually identifying themselves as evangelicals. But a few are in a no-man's land, leaving confused those who try to make strict religious classifications.

The mother Church then pulled in its reins, obligating the remaining groups to sing songs to Mary and prohibiting Protestants from addressing them. At a large charismatic stadium rally in Costa Rica the archbishop pointedly reminded participants that Mary was with the Apostles in the upper room when Pentecost occurred.

Whatever contact there was between the Gospel People and the Catholic charismatics is now all but broken off at the group level. Many evangelicals never did recognize the Catholic *carismáticos* as fellow believers. There are lingering concerns. A Catholic sings a song of worship to Mary in a charismatic meeting. How many contradictions can be tolerated? Many Catholic charismatics, however, have had a genuine experience with Christ and show evidences of spiritual fruit in their lives.

A Resurrection Parish

Up against the hills to the south of Mexico City is a poor neighborhood where Father Alfonso Navarro leads the ministries of the Resurrection Parish. His testimony is evangelical and he invites Protestant organizations to join him in evangelizing the people. With the blessing of the bishop, his Center of Evangelization and Religious Instruction conducts seminars to involve other Catholic parishes in evangelizing Latin America.

While some foreign and international Protestant groups have accepted Navarro's invitation to work in the Resurrection Parish, most local Mexican evangelicals will have nothing to do with the operation.

But scattered across the continent are groups like *Arbol de la Vida* ("Tree of Life") in Costa Rica where evangelicals and Roman Catholics fellowship together. In El Salvador Baptists, Lutherans and Catholics work closely helping the war refugees and ministering to the needs of the poor.

We can get excited about all these cooperative developments. But they are isolated, few and far between at the present time. The sad fact is that the Catholic Church is now calling the Protestant groups "sects," an increasingly used epithet.

The Faith of the Charcoal Seller

Noted Spanish philosopher and author, Miguel de Unamuno, recounts the fable of the charcoal seller who was asked "What do you believe?" He replies, "I believe what the Church believes." When asked, "What does the Church believe?" his answer is "Ah, it believes what I believe."

With all the reports of the various developments in Latin Roman Catholicism, we must be reminded that many Latin Americans are still the charcoal sellers. Many enter church only for their marriage and the two times they are carried in — as children to be baptized, and in a coffin for the funeral. The furniture in the sanctuary has been moved, the mass is in Spanish or Portuguese, the priest faces the congregation across a communion table. Otherwise, for the average Catholic almost everything is the same.

David Barrett estimates that of the 369 million Catholics in Latin America, there are only 2 million "Catholic Pentecostals." (*World Christian Encyclopedia*). There are no more than 1.5 million Catholics participating in the CEBs. Many more millions do not.

Never the Same Again

Archbishop Oscar Romero is remembered as the "voice of the voiceless." There is no turning back the clock in Latin America. A great social revolution grinds on. The Bible, now open to millions, is causing its own revolution. The resulting cracks in the Roman Catholic Church will never be repaired. But, interesting as these developments all may be, the fact remains that the vast majority of Latin America's peoples need to be evangelized and discipled.

SUGGESTED FURTHER READING:

- Edward L. Cleary *Crisis and Change, The Church in Latin America Today* (Orbis Books of Maryknoll, New York, 1985). An excellent, somewhat optimistic description of the Latin American Roman Catholic Church by a Dominican priest.

- Gustavo Gutiérrez *We Drink from Our Own Wells* (The Spiritual Journey of a People) (SCM Press of London, 1984 — Spanish original, 1983). Foreword is written by Henri Nouwen. A presentation of the "spirituality of liberation" which intends to help provide a Biblical and spiritual foundation.

- Guillermo Cook *The Expectation of the Poor* (Orbis Books of Maryknoll, New York, 1985). A comprehensive study of the Latin American Base Ecclesial Communities in Brazil from a Protestant perspective.

- For the reader in Spanish: Samuel Escobar *La fe evangélica y las teologías de la liberación* (Casa Bautista de Publicaciones of El Paso, 1987). A stimulating work which assists Latin evangelicals in appraising liberation thought while developing important subjects for a Latin American evangelical theology.

CHAPTER THIRTEEN

Not what we expected

Enter a large Latin American evangelical church and one thing you may note is an uneven floor. You can distinguish changes in the tile patterns in one or more places. The building has undergone numerous additions with the congregation's growth. Large paintings or murals grace the walls. In one of these, Christians are rising to meet Christ at His Second Coming. Another is that of an open Bible on a rock withstanding the boisterous waves of worldly forces.

The congregation sings the same chorus for ten or fifteen minutes. The song leader grasps the microphone in one hand and the other arm is stretched untiringly upward.

The sermon is simple and invariably concludes with an altar call; streams of people move forward. Some may be responding to the Gospel for the first time, others coming for reconciliation, for physical healing, or for the resolution of a spiritual burden. There is something reminiscent of traditional liturgies where there is always confession, reconciliation with God, and the granting of His peace.

There is no missionary in sight, and a visitor may feel that North America is left far behind. This is a church of the fifth wave, one with little or no history of organizational relationship with a foreign denomination or mission board.

The Alliance for Progress and the economic systems which gave so much hope failed, according to most Latin American analysts. Society has come apart. The Roman Catholic Church had its plans to re-establish itself, but it has been fractured, each of its pieces moving in a different direction. What about the Gospel People?

Perhaps of all places in the world, this is where the evangelical movement has flourished — unevenly, to be sure, but expanding

Thriving evangelical congregations in Peru (above) and Mexico (below)

rapidly. There are at least 40 million evangelicals in Latin America. They are doubling in number every four years in some Central American countries.

But it did not turn out as we had expected.

Worship to a Latin Beat

The hymnals translated into Spanish have been generally discarded in favor of choruses with a Latin beat. Many pastors who took training in pastoral theology are preaching in half-empty churches while crowds flock to hear the charismatic pastor who may practice a profession Monday through Friday. Traditional patterns of church life revolving around the Sunday School and the Women's Class give way to praise services, healing meetings and all-night vigils. Many traditional denominational churches have adopted a Pentecostal style without changing their theology. That church where you hear people clapping as they sing — it may be Presbyterian.

There are still plenty of sedate denominational congregations and churches where a residue of missionary influence and style prevails. But the 10% of Mexico City's churches that are growing fastest are drawing more new people than all the rest put together. And most of these churches are Pentecostal. These large fifth wave churches in Chile are larger than all the other types combined. Granted, the original denomination of the various Chilean Pentecostal churches broke from the Methodists in 1909, but that former link is only history now.

On top of the previous four waves of evangelical advance — the immigrant churches, the main-line denominations, the faith missions and the newer denominations — the *fifth wave* emerges. Sprouting from Latin American soil itself, they include such groups as the Brazil for Christ movement and the Rose of Sharon groups in Central America.

While a missionary is still trying to wean his church away from foreign subsidies and encourage his people to take more initiative, down the street the Christian butcher begins a preaching service in his home singing to the accompaniment of guitars and maracas. There is no missionary to remind him that the service should be over at 9 o'clock or that the message should have three points. Cats and dogs wander underfoot and the children are noisy until they fall asleep. But the heart burden of the poor is poured out with tears and shouts.

The group becomes too large for the lay-pastor's living room, so it moves out to the patio under a covering of palm branches. And then, through incredible personal sacrifice — every peso goes for another bag of cement — a chapel is built. Before the cement is dry or the window frames installed, the group is concerned about a nearby squatters village where there is no witness. That is considered a *campo blanco*, a "whitened field," where a branch preaching point must be established. When such preaching points become daughter congregations, the network becomes a new denomination.

Why do people elsewhere know so little about these fifth wave churches? It is only natural that Baptist missionaries return home to report on Baptist work, and Alliance missionaries about the Alliance churches. It seems no one has any reason to report on what in some countries is the biggest wave yet.

All is not well in the Latin American churches, however. Before discussing their problems and needs, it is time to answer the first question posted at the beginning of the book.

What Makes Them Grow?

1. *A background of Christian knowledge already acquired in the Roman Catholic tradition.* Witnessing Christians in Latin America do not usually have to start at square one explaining who Jesus is.

2. *A world view that still accepts the supernatural.* While this is often misdirected, a witnessing Christian can redirect a person's faith to Christ.

3. *Disenchantment with the Roman Catholic Church.* Among the reasons for a Catholic to leave the fold are:
   - Lack of priests and pastoral care;
   - Contradictions discovered between the Church's teachings and the Bible;
   - Moral failure of some clergy;
   - Identification of the Church with the establishment (or sometimes the opposite: its identification with the revolutionaries).

4. *Religious liberty.* The Roman Catholic Church still exercises great political power in many countries. Protestants, in effect, are only tolerated. Missionary visas may be hard to obtain in many countries and there are subtle forms of social discrimination. Street services are

illegal in Mexico (but in the shadow of the Benito Juárez monument in the Alameda Central Park in Mexico City on Sunday afternoons there are large evangelical street services). Problems, yes. But enough liberty for the Gospel to take root in the hearts of people.

5. *Poverty and insecurity.* These are conditions which lead people not only to Christian communities where there is love and acceptance, but also to Christ, the ultimate source of strength in trouble.

6. *Evangelical use of mass media.* Rising literacy coincides with the wide distribution of easy-to-read versions of the Scripture. The fact that there are evangelical radio stations in each Central American country is a partial explanation of the phenomenal evangelical growth there. The electronic church, too, has brought the attention of millions to the Gospel. But many culturally sensitive Latins are not impressed by the entertainment glitter of many U.S.-originated telecasts, not to speak of the scandals associated with some of these ministries.

7. *Evangelical church structure.* While some traditional denominations still limit preaching and presiding over the Lord's Supper to ordained seminary graduates, groups that are growing have actively encouraged the lay-pastor and given him authority. Or a layman starts preaching and establishes a church without asking anyone's permission. Communications theory supports the concept that people are persuaded more often by others of their own kind. That lay-pastor who is a storekeeper may be more convincing in explaining the Gospel to another merchant than someone more removed.

8. *Mobilization.* The Evangelism-in-Depth concept mentioned earlier, where all Christians are encouraged to tell their friends about Christ, is operative in many evangelical communities. Typical mass evangelism attempts to multiply the audience for an evangelist. The mobilization concept attempts to multiply the evangelists.

9. *Faith in God's power.* The mobilization concept is an undeniable formula for growth. But if it is accepted cerebrally — no one can deny that it is logical — it is not enough. People can be trained to witness and be exhorted to do so, but the ordinary person, Latin American or otherwise, is nervous and embarrassed, afraid he or she will say the wrong thing. Most churches will give lip-service to mobilization, but nothing happens.

The Pentecostal churches are often the ones in which mobilization really takes place. Theirs is a theology which empowers believers. People know that God will answer prayer about the person to whom they expect to witness, and they know that the Holy Spirit will give the witnessing Christian the words to say and take away their timidity. Of course, the Pentecostals do not have a monopoly on these truths.

10. *Contextualization.* Just as the Apostle Paul was "Jew to the Jews, gentile to the gentiles," so the gospel expressed in Latin America must fit into its surroundings.

If *salsa* is the prevailing rhythm on the pop music radio show, it becomes the beat to which choruses are sung in church. Unison praying — each worshipper pleading to God regarding his or her personal needs — is more common than overly intellectual expositions. Worship forms and organization are spontaneous and personal rather than rigid and overly-programmed.

11. *The critical mass.* When there are only a dozen evangelicals in a city, as faithful as they may be in telling their friends about Christ and inviting them to church, growth will be slow in absolute terms. They only have so many friends and so many hours in a day. But if 10% of a city's people are actively witnessing — 10,000 believers in a city of 100,000 — hardly a person will not have some contact with that 10,000. The numbers grow like compound interest and, for the time being, the curves on the graphs get steeper. In many areas of Latin America this critical mass has been reached. We could not stop the movement even if we wanted to.

12. *A straightforward message.* "*Solo Cristo Salva*" ("Only Christ saves") is a common motto for campaigns, stickers, posters, or even graffiti. During the Evangelism-in-Depth movement in Bolivia believers placed oil drums across the face of a barren mountain side in full view of La Paz, the capital. At night the drums were lit, spelling out the message in flames: Solo Cristo Salva. There is no compromise regarding salvation — it is only through Christ. Repentance and faith in Him is the first step. The Bible is the book. This is simplistic to many, but for desperate people looking for straightforward answers, the Gospel People show they have no doubts about what to say.

In Honduras, during one period, the number of evangelical churches grew at about 16% a year. In Guatemala evangelicals talk about having gained between 25 and 30% of the population. Many, of course, will point out that mission and the work of a pastor is more than just numbers and percentages. But tracking numerical growth does have a basis in the book of Acts. And growth in quantity very often develops out of groups where there has been qualitative growth.

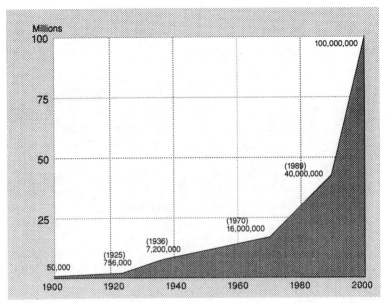

Latin American Evangelical Church Growth, 1900 to 2000. Estimates by William Taylor.

The Flames Are Spreading

Pedro Paredes had come from Peru to Costa Rica to study, made Central America his home, founded and became pastor of a large, thriving church. During a missionary conference he shared a conviction that had come to him during a recent visit to his home country. After 46 years God called him back to the jungles of Peru's Amazonia.

For years Chilean missionaries have been evangelizing Peru while Guatemalans planted churches in other Central American countries. But this kind of missionary work is much like Iowans planting churches in Montana, among people of their same language and culture. Learning Indian languages or crossing the sea to another continent was something only gringos did.

Latin America has lagged behind Africa and Asia in sending out cross-cultural missionaries. But this has changed in the last ten years. Delegates from all Latin world countries gathered in Sao Paulo, Brazil in 1987 for the Congress of Missions of Ibero-America (COMIBAM) to challenge each other to share the good news with the

Mission outreach in a "red light district", San José, Costa Rica by the Brazilian Deus es Amor *Church which has established outreach in Central and South America.*

entire world. At this event Latin America, which has often been referred to as a mission *field*, was clearly identified as a mission *force*. National agencies are on the rise. Major efforts by Brazilians are leading the way.

FEMEDEC (Federation of Costa Rican Evangelical Missions), a Costa Rican missionary society, in its first four years of existence has become the vehicle for missions outreach for 16 denominations and has already sent out 13 people to Spain, East Asia and the Mid-East. This tiny country has adopted 61 unreached "people groups" to evangelize.

The Latin American church's missionary zeal is uniting with that of churches from other parts of the world to carry out the Great Commission.

Talking about these unexpected developments — new forms of church life, phenomenal growth in numbers, and Latin American missionary outreach — with a prominent Latin American church leader, his reaction was: "Isn't that the way God always works — doing the unexpected?"

SUGGESTED FURTHER READINGS:

- Larry D. Pate *From Every People* (MARC of Monrovia, CA, 1989). This is a handbook of Two-Thirds World missions with directory, histories, and analysis. Pages 275-301 deal with Latin America.

CHAPTER FOURTEEN

The flip side of success

North Americans are quick to note how strong (if not dictatorial) Latin American heads of government are, how top-down the managerial styles in Latin businesses, or how macho and domineering is the father of the family. "How can we expect the churches and their pastors to be different?" we ask.

Some observers trace this authoritarianism to insecurity. The lay pastor who is a butcher without any theological training fears that his members will forsake him for a more attractive church. He may demand that no member attend any meeting other than those of his congregation.

But society is changing. University students study in settings where there is dialogue, where questions may be asked. Openness and dialogue may be typical of university settings, but how about common people who just want to be preached at? The Catholic Base Church Communities have demonstrated that under the right conditions, the poor and the uneducated want to and can participate in serious discussions about the Christian faith.

Living by Do's and Don'ts

Legalism is a handmaiden of authoritarianism. Many an evangelical woman will never be seen in slacks or with makeup, nor will she shape her hair, leaving it straight and long. New, first-generation Christians may be forgiven for certain legalisms, but some churches never liberate their people from the "don'ts".

Some fifth wave groups have adopted an almost Old Testament lifestyle under the law, like a group in Chile that, among other practices, celebrates the annual Feast of the Tabernacles, taking the congregation out of the city to camp in makeshift shelters in obedience to Jewish law.

Legalism enshrines practices that may have been valid at one time, but then locks a church into a pattern that is irrelevant for a new generation. In some Chilean churches women's groups are often called "Dorcas Societies", an appropriate name. The very mention of the fact that in another church a women's group bore another name is met with unbelief. The name "Dorcas" had become enshrined, legalized.

We smile at this, but the fact that many churches are not growing is due to this kind of mentality. Meetings seven nights a week might have been in order for new Christians who needed support in the face of persecution or who, because they were illiterate, could not read the Word for themselves at home. But this plays havoc with family life.

The members of a missionary family assigned to a church in Mexico found themselves locked into a schedule of services every night of the week with no time for their children or outreach. Only severe illness could justify their absence, and the pastor's word was final.

In one Mexican home a meeting was announced. Only about five were present, but a stand was brought out, the leader stood behind it and in all seriousness led us through a miniature church service, with the Scripture readings and prayers in proper order. The mechanical imitation of form, in one way or another, is seen everywhere. What should have been an opportunity for small group interaction and responding to personal problems in an intimate setting were lost.

Becoming Just a Number

"Massification" — dealing with people as a part of a great mass instead of attending to their individual needs — is a temptation that often follows success. Many pastors deal with the crowd and not with the individual.

After the nation-wide Evangelism-in-Depth movements of the 1960s, the Latin America Mission coordinators of these movements realized that something was missing. Thousands of new Christians were coming into the churches, but no one was personally taking the individual converts to help them with their problems. Therefore, the concept of believers taking responsibility to disciple new Christians has been the emphasis of the In-depth Institute (International Institute of In-Depth Evangelization) for the past several years. People are starved for personal concern and love in many Latin American churches.

Roman Catholics who have learned something about spiritual sharing in the small Base Communities have said to evangelicals who have been successfully capturing the crowds and erecting large buildings, "You seem to be going to where we have just come from."

Preaching Only John 3:16

"They preach from only five or six texts," critics say about some of the large churches in Chile. "Reductionism", or reducing the gospel to only a few texts, or to certain topics such as healing, is another weakness in many churches. Some groups view all illness, psychological or physical, as demon possession and their major activity is exorcism.

Outside these churches systems are breaking down. The local factory is firing all its workers every 13 weeks and rehiring them to avoid paying social security and other workers' benefits. Young people are joining the guerrillas. Deforestation is causing erosion that results in contaminated water. But in most evangelical churches pastors say little that will enlighten the members about their responsibility in situations demanding justice, Christian discernment about political issues or environmental concerns.

Some leaders who touch such broader concerns, especially if they enter the political arena, may be dubbed followers of Liberation Theology. Liberationists are feared so much that preaching social responsibility, even within the most evangelical framework, will mark a person as dangerous in some circles.

And those who have social concerns tend to stereotype the others as "pietists" — interested only in their personal relationship with God, with no concern for neighbor. They often overlook the fact that many "pietists" reach out to help without preaching about it.

A House Divided

For years, because missionaries of the mainline denominations in

Latin America tended to come from the evangelical wing of their denominations, and the churches they worked with were also evangelical, the Gospel People were united. The mainline groups worked together with the people from the other waves in united evangelistic and other efforts. But now the movement is divided into two major streams.

In one stream are those with broad social and ecumenical concern. Some are committed to Liberation Theology, their principal theme being the radical change of political structures. Others in the same stream are winning people to Christ along with their social ministries. Here we find most traditional denominations and the ecumenical agencies along with a few fifth wave church groups. They may affiliate with the Latin American Council of Churches, CLAI.

In the other stream are most of the churches related to the faith missions, the newer denominations and most of the Pentecostals and independent churches. This more conservative current tends to relate to CONELA, a Latin American fellowship of evangelicals.

There have been painful splits in denominations, churches and Christian ministries in the process. Some groups, however, remain blissfully unaware of these tensions, and the vast majority belong to neither CLAI nor CONELA. Some take advantage of the services of both, while remaining independent.

But then there is also the inevitable fragmentation: divisions due to personalities, churches breaking away from heavy-handed missionary organizations, and the usual doctrinal issues. We may also mention a kind of Latin individualism that frustrated Simon Bolivar, the South American liberator. While proposing to unite all the new Latin American republics he realized that such an effort was like "plowing the sea".

Alliances of evangelicals in many countries have developed only because of external threat, when religious liberty has been endangered. In Nicaragua there was no such alliance until the 1972 Managua earthquake forced the Christians to work together to distribute relief supplies. It is no wonder that government officials throw up their hands in trying to deal with this amorphous collection of "sects", and the Catholics point to our lack of unity as proof that they are the only true church.

The picture is not all dismal. Some ministries like the Bible societies, World Vision, Latin America Mission and others have been able to span the gulf and work with Christians on all sides. The Latin American Theological Fraternity (FTL), too, has been bringing together leaders, theologically evangelical, from both sides.

Watch That Back Door

Young people attending a church pastored by a dentist begin to leave because his style of ministry and the content of the message do not answer their questions, and so they end up in a no man's land. Campus ministries are frustrated because the students they win to Christ are uncomfortable in many of the churches.

Studies in Mexico City indicate there are only half as many Protestants in the churches as there are registered in the census. The fact that the government lists as Protestants all the sects (such as Jehovah's Witnesses and the Mormons) accounts for part of the difference. But there is a growing awareness that across the years people have left the evangelical churches, while still identifying themselves as "Protestant" to the census taker at the door. In other words, we are seeing the beginnings of a "nominalism" that is common in traditionally Protestant countries.

There is so much concern about bringing people in the front door of the church that evangelicals fail to see the exodus out the back door. Many who leave maintain a personal evangelical faith, but they haven't found a church that addresses their particular problems. Fortunately, there are some churches now that do.

More disappointing is one survey which shows that there is a substantial number of Catholics identifying themselves as "former Protestant" in one country.

Much of the Gospel People's advance has rested on the demonstration of God's power in healing the sick, making sober the alcoholic, and cleansing those who are really oppressed by demonic spirits. Such "power encounters," the visible side of spiritual warfare, continue to convince thousands.

But as Christian university students face intellectual challenges to the gospel and as believers probe the foundations of their faith, the need increases for "truth encounters" with the Word of God. Few pastors prepare their young people for the ideological discussions that arise even at the high school level in Latin America. Solid Biblical training would stop some of the flow through the back door.

That flow also shows a lack of serious "commitment encounter" with Christ. There is no lack of committing, it seems, when we see believers go forward over and over again at the call of repentance. But the evangelical movement still suffers a lack of spiritual depth and stability. Millions who are turning to the gospel in Latin America need to establish a growing relationship with Christ, His Word, and His people.

Competition in the Spiritual Marketplace

Compounding the problems of the Gospel People is the newly competitive religious "market". Well-scrubbed young men in white shirts and ties scour the middle-class neighborhoods on behalf of the Mormons. The insistent house-to-house visitation by the Jehovah's Witnesses has made this evangelistic method unacceptable in many places. New Age publications are in the bookstores. In some countries the Hare Krishnas and the Children of God have come and gone.

One enemy of the Gospel People is old, and yet constantly renewing itself: spiritism. North Americans may consider it a primitive, rural religion, remembering what they have heard about Haitian voodoo or animistic Indian practices. But it is a pervasive influence in every country — at least 40% of the Brazilian population practices some form of spiritism.

A Brazilian bookstore distributing books exclusively about spiritism with samples of the title covers.

No shingle outside the door announces the services of the fortune teller in Costa Rica, but the line of people waiting for an appointment on the porch outside is a clue that people still trust in someone to cast a spell on their enemies. The way the scissors are left on someone's table is for them more than a superstitious habit. The withered flowers at the base of a statue to María Loanza, a pagan goddess, on the median strip of one of the Caracas expressways indicate that some people risked their lives crossing the traffic lanes to make their offering to her. Presidents and peasants alike see no contradiction between their Catholic faith and an appeal to a pagan spirit world.

The building down the street in Sao Paulo, Brazil, a spiritist's meeting place, tells us that spiritism is institutionalized.

North Americans may dismiss all this as nonsense, but most Gospel People take the spirit world seriously. While some groups are extreme ("pray that the spirit of hiccups will depart"), most evangelicals will believe that the local fortune-teller or witch does manipulate demonic spirits as they are described Biblically. An international witches congress in Bogotá, Colombia, is an occasion for serious prayer by evangelical Christians there. A house formerly occupied by someone involved in witchcraft will require a special service of prayer to cleanse it of any residual territorial spirits.

New missionaries, fully educated in U.S. seminaries, may find themselves at a loss when local believers ask them to pray for deliverance of people from demonic possession. Those with at least some idea about "spiritual warfare" will fare better.

The Gospel People are multiplying. But their struggle is far from over.

CHAPTER FIFTEEN

Warmth from
the Gulf Stream

The beaches of Long Island and Cape Cod are warmed by waters that were heated in that boiler which is the Gulf of Mexico. It is this same current, the Gulf Stream, that keeps Ireland green and the rest of Western Europe inhabitable, even though much of it shares the same latitude as Labrador.

Is there more of anything from Latin America to bless our shores?

In the lobby of many a Latin American airport stands the bust of Alberto Santos-Dumont to remind travelers that one of the early aviation pioneers was a Brazilian. We admire the Caribbean baseball heroes in our major leagues and Pelé, the Brazilian soccer star. We read the translated work of Gabriel García Márquez and other writers and enjoy the beat of Latin music. Whether it be coffee or bananas, Venezuelan petroleum or Mexican silver, our lives are enriched by Latin Americans and their products.

The experience of Latin American Christians developed on the front lines of spiritual battle and surrounded by the pain of Third World living, is also a source of encouragement and insights for the churches in the rest of the world. The "mother church-daughter church" or "sending church-receiving church" mentality is giving way to an openness to learn from the Gospel People and from Christians of other cultures as well. The major contributions from Latin American churches are the following.

Everyone with a Paddle

Two dug-out canoes, hollowed from a tree trunk, with passengers sitting in a row, are on their way up a river. Cartoon sketches of such canoes were used in flip-charts illustrating concepts of Evangelism-in-Depth. In the first sketch the canoe's pilot, sitting in back, is the only one with a paddle. The rest of the occupants are passengers, passive and uninvolved. In the second canoe everyone has a paddle. Which canoe will go faster? The next step comes easily, explaining that the church in which everyone ministers, is the one which will move faster.

As mentioned earlier, leaders of the Latin America Mission spent the better part of a decade — the 1950s — analyzing evangelistic methods and experimenting with mass campaigns. After studying such disparate groups as the Assemblies of God, the Communist Party, and Jehovah's Witnesses, LAM leaders sensed the common denominator for expansion was the ability to motivate to a strong commitment and to involve actively the total membership of the group. Everyone had to paddle.

What emerged from Evangelism-in-Depth was a conviction that

Lay people meet together right where they live to receive training for outreach in the 1967 Peruvian Evangelism-in-Depth efforts.

"the successful expansion of any movement is in direct proportion to its success in mobilizing and occupying its total membership in constant propagation of its beliefs." The Biblical basis for this principle was found in Ephesians 4 where the task of the apostles, prophets, evangelists, pastors and teachers is "to prepare God's people for works of service."

The concept of mobilizing lay people has spread in many forms and shapes. In many cases, they are stimulated and encouraged by the experience in Latin America's laboratory.

The impact of the E/D movement throughout the 1960s and early 1970s and continuing on in various expressions until today is significant for all of the work of the Lord in Latin America. It is the Biblically-based principle of the mobilization of the laity. Nothing is more basic in the work and outreach of the church.

Thatched Roof Pastoral Training

In coastal Colombia *burros* still carry burdens in the village streets lined by adobe houses with thatched roofs and dugout canoes still ply the rivers. A grass-roots movement when thousands turned to Christ in the 1950s and 1960s took place within the vast area served by the Association of Evangelical Churches of Colombia (AIEC).

Leader Gregorio Landero became particularly concerned by a 1980 survey of his denomination. It revealed that 80% of the pastors in the AIEC had not finished their primary school education and the same number did not have any formal Biblical or pastoral training.

Many pastors were farmers or tradesmen in remote villages, some in areas controlled by guerrilla forces or drug lords. They could not leave their families, farms or businesses to study in a residential Bible institute.

These staggering figures stirred the denominational leadership to establish the Pastoral Training Program in 1981. In ten years, more than 2000 church leaders have studied in a comprehensive program which mainly utilizes extension methods and materials, often combining them with other types of education.

TEE (Theological Education by Extension) was also developed in Latin America's laboratory, among the Presbyterians in Guatemala, as mentioned earlier.

In Colombia the program was adapted to a four-tier program with the following results in ten years:

— *Primary education* through a Christian adult education program approved by the Colombian government. There were 450 graduates.

— A four year *Certificate level Biblical studies* program by extension. There were 1600 graduates and 600 currently studying.

— A three year *Diploma level* by extension for pastors and key church leaders. There were 90 graduates, 80 currently enrolled.

— A *Seminary level* provision for those qualifying to study at the Biblical Seminary in Medellín. This has produced 14 graduates and currently 11 are studying.

During the ten years, the AIEC continued to make giant strides in numerical growth. This presents an even greater need for leadership training so that new churches and new people can be attended to. From 1985 to 1990, AIEC church membership nearly doubled, increasing from 11,600 to 20,000.

Here is a church which made a realistic study of its situation and took concrete steps to meet its need for leadership training. Other groups are doing the same.

This account of a church — only one of many — which realistically assessed the situation and then, took action to begin meeting critical training needs is encouraging indeed.

TEE, in this case, was more than simply taking the seminary professor to the village. The kind of flexibility in theological education demonstrated in the AIEC is seen in downtown evening seminaries. In the back room of a city church cab drivers and pharmacists are studying the Word. There are church leaders who could never get into a residential day program, even if it were available.

There are hundreds of denominations and groups of churches in Latin America which are not aware of the need, or if conscious of it, do not know how to meet it. This is particularly true of many of the teeming fifth wave churches. TEE provides one valuable source of help for them.

Back to Medellín

Twenty years after Liberation Theology was launched in Medellín, Colombia, a group of Latin American evangelical leaders from eleven countries met in the same Andean city in 1988, to look at it afresh from a Biblical perspective. The initial shock wave of Liberation

Theology — of priests and pastors committing themselves to radical political change and L.T.'s revolutionary new theological vocabulary — had long since passed. The group was critical of the lack of attention in L.T. to personal regeneration and repentance. They were critical of "what Liberation theologians do to the Bible" — liberation principles of interpretation. But the document the group produced was mainly one of confession and commitment.

They confessed that Latin evangelicals have too often "conformed to the structures, values and norms of the society." They confessed: "Many of us have not been concerned for the poor, the marginalized, mistreated and needy, as an expression of our mission: we have taken this to be [only] an optional concern."

And they committed themselves, among other things, to "developing concrete programs that could have a social impact from a Biblical perspective," "developing a way of discipleship that can prepare believers for wholeness of service in the world," and "seeking justice, not in order to bring in the kingdom, but as an expression of its presence in our midst."

Liberation Theology can provide valuable insights to Latin evangelical churches in spite of its *obvious flaws*, such as:

- Being part and parcel of a Roman Catholicism which seeks to encompass all of society without much concern about the world's contamination by sin.

- Basing its reality in the struggle between capital and labor, between industrial countries and underdeveloped poor nations, and virtually ignoring the Biblical focus of an ultimate struggle between God and Satan.

- Emphasizing disproportionately that the poor are a product only of inequitable distribution of goods, at the expense of other related Biblical truths such as man's alienation from God because of sin.

- The selective use of Scripture, interpreting the Bible according to a predetermined ideology, in this case Marxist.

So, in what ways can such a flawed Liberation Theology contribute to the Gospel People? We can suggest several:

(1) The devastating poverty in which the majority of Latin Americans live, and on which the liberationists focus, should become the evangelicals' burden as well. This concern for the poor

enriches our understanding and application of the Scriptures and helps *us* become less selective in our use of it.

(2)   Liberation Theology also makes the Kingdom of God visible to Latin Americans. The Gospel People need to be reminded that there is life on this side of the grave as well as life beyond it. In preaching the gospel there should also be concern about justice and equity and an effort to overcome oppression and poverty.

(3)   Liberation theologians reject Western philosophical emphases in traditional theology in favor of pointing up the influence of modern history and the social sciences. Western philosophy has impacted greatly our reading of the Scriptures. What Latin evangelicals need is a fresh study of the Bible in their context.

(4)   Liberation Theology traces its roots to many continents. But its greatest development has been in Latin America where it arose. It can stimulate the evangelical to "leave the balcony" and "descend into the street" where the people are.

Small Is Beautiful

The small group of Roman Catholic workers meeting in a squatters' settlement in Brazil looks surprisingly "Protestant" to many observers. This closely-knit CEB group says, in effect, "the true church is not every baptized Catholic within the parish boundaries; it is the "gathered" church, those who are really committed." This is a very Protestant concept, along with the CEB groups' freedom to give everyone a voice to share what the Bible passage means to each one.

The small group, with its greater sense of community, mutual sharing and sense of belonging, is nothing new to many evangelical churches. But this is revolutionary in much of the Roman Catholic world. The "gathered church" nature and the freedom of expression in the CEBs are similar to some of the evangelical Fifth Wave churches.

Add to this the social activities of the CEBs not often seen in evangelical churches. These are no longer the passive and fatalistic traditional Catholics. These people learn to speak, to read, to relate, to organize. They have a strong link between belief and action.

These CEBs still look very Roman Catholic to evangelicals. They are usually in the stream of Liberation Theology. Guillermo Cook, who has studied them carefully, predicted that they would shake Latin America and the rest of the Third World. Their impact may have been made and now they may be declining, says Cook. With the Vatican taking a harder line against Liberation Theology and those in that stream, many CEB members may be crossing over to evangelical groups. _____

The Gospel People are living under the impact of these dynamic influences in Latin America. We, too, may find in them emerging answers to the questions of churches elsewhere.

SUGGESTED FURTHER READINGS:

- Kenneth Mulholland *Adventures in Training the Ministry* — A Honduran Case Study in Theological Education by Extension (Presbyterian and Reformed Publishing House, 1976). This work on TEE is an example of how a development on theological education, originating in Latin America, has been adopted as a missionary strategy in many parts of the world.

- W. Dayton Roberts (Editor) *Liberation Theology: An Evangelical Assessment* (MARC Publications of Monrovia, CA, 1987). "An easy-to-read, easy-to-understand case study about the Theologies of Liberation and their impact on Christianity in Latin America," with seven other contributors.

CHAPTER SIXTEEN

Is Christ the answer?

"Christ is the Answer" has become a slogan for many an evangelistic campaign, a title for a Gospel tract, and an inspiration for a Christian graffiti artist. Sometimes a cynic scribbles underneath: "What is the question?"

The question is all around us in Latin America. How can countries so rich in gold, silver, oil and other resources be so poor? How can lives destroyed by alcohol and drugs be recovered? Who can bring peace in the battle between revolutionaries and oppressors?

But "Christ as the Answer" can be interpreted in a number of ways.

Win Them One By One

Conversion of individuals is without question the way most Gospel People interpret Christ as-the-answer. Continuing up-beat evangelism is not just a fire-escape to heaven. Regenerate people create a climate and a force for good in society. When Juan, the neighborhood drunk, becomes a sober, steady, sincere and loving husband and parent, and a responsible worker and citizen, society is changed too in some small measure.

But the reports about Latin America's fantastic church growth and the sight of some of the large evangelical churches may mislead us to think that not many Pedros and Marías are left to be evangelized.

The growth of the Gospel People has been uneven. 30% of Guatemala's population may be evangelical, but in Uruguay it may be less than 2%. Entire villages are evangelical in southern Mexico, but vast areas are unreached in the country's heartland.

An evangelical "cathedral" and other large churches serve the poor in Santiago, Chile, but precious little is done among the middle and upper classes. Maracaibo, Venezuela's second city, has a sizeable evangelical population but the capital, Caracas, has been expensive and forbiddingly secular for missionaries.

Arab, Chinese, Japanese and Jewish minorities have been generally untouched in Latin America. In many cities the poorest of the poor, the rich elites, the university students, the intelligentsia and the drug crowd are still unreached and they would be uncomfortable in the evangelical church that Juan attends.

Computer Science and Fishing Boats

A large tent rises on the edge of Mexico City where middle-class suburbia has spread out and collides with the poor, almost rural older settlers. Inside, about 3000 people sing to the beat of electronic instruments led by a half-dozen women with tambourines.

This is the Calacoaya Cultural Center, founded by Gonzalo Vega, who, with his wife, began studying the Bible in their home, stimulated by the Catholic charismatic movement. They accepted Christ and in 1976 started a home group with 8 people which soon swelled to 70. For two years they rented a house for meetings, but opposition from neighbors forced them out. For a year they met in various locations. When the attendance reached 120 they left Catholicism and Vega quit his job in advertising to dedicate all his time to the group.

Their first building with a capacity of 500 soon proved inadequate so they erected a huge tent. About 1500 attended the first tent meeting, but that was already too small. Women were given seats while the men stood. Since then, the tent has been expanded.

But the Calacoaya Center has added another dimension to offering Christ as the answer. In addition to winning people to Christ, classes are offered to help church members and neighbors get better jobs. This is no mere basket-weaving program. These are serious courses in English, French, electricity and computer science. The monthly bulletin is a wealth of information about mechanical, medical and buy-and-sell services with updates on some 60 ministries of this group which serve not only the congregation but the surrounding community as well.

In Colombia a group of fishermen need a boat. An enterprising Colombian sees the need for public transportation into a new *barrio* which needs bus service. AGAPE, a Colombian Christian development organization, not only loans money for these businesses but also provides to these Colombians management counsel and instruction in accounting so that the businesses can turn a profit. A Canadian missionary started AGAPE when he realized many Christians were so poor that they were hardly surviving, let alone having money to support their churches.

Money down the drain? Hardly. The combination of management training plus available capital make these people good risks. AGAPE of Colombia is part of a network of similar organizations knit together loosely by Opportunity International. The parallel organization in Costa Rica reports that 13% of the borrowers are behind in maintaining repayment schedules. But this is nothing less than phenomenal in a country where 72% of all borrowers are in arrears on loan repayments.

In many countries, the Salvation Army, World Relief, World Vision and other international agencies, including many more traditional mission organizations, are participating directly in social outreach. In the process, Latin American churches and denominations have become involved as well. It is also heartening to see Central

Children in a Bible class for abandoned children at an evangelical orphanage in a huge metropolitan area

American evangelicals respond significantly across national borders to relief needs caused by earthquakes, volcanic eruptions, floods, or political upheavals and war.

But all of this is nothing more than a drop in the bucket when measured by the potential of the Gospel People or by the enormity of the need.

Making a Difference in the Market Place

Downwind from an enormous foul-smelling dump just outside Mexico City, is a town which is slowly emerging from a squatters' village status. The streets are still unpaved. An unfenced canal full of factory waste runs through town, creating a hazard for children. An outreach program of social work from the local Presbyterian church is modest. What is remarkable is that this effort is part of a network of projects started by former evangelical university students, now Mexican pro-

Foreman and engineer, both evangelicals, oversee massive public works project in Mexico City to convert 375 acres of a former dump to recreational areas.

fessionals with better than average incomes. They took seriously their Christian responsibility for the poor and formed AMEXTRA, a home-grown Christian Mexican development organization.

Even John Wesley lamented the fact that as God helped Christians prosper, they tended to become materialistic and lose their love for God and neighbor. Among the Gospel People is a growing college-educated second generation, rising socially. Some, like those of Wesley's generation, grow cold in their Christian faith. But there are groups of Latin American Christian businessmen who encourage each other to witness in their circles. Changes in society come about when Christians take their places responsibly in government, education, communications, management and labor, and in the arts.

As they join the middle-class consumer society, many of them forget their roots — the poor *barrio* where they grew up and found Christ in the neighborhood storefront church. Some urban evangelical churches are installing carpets in the aisles and providing robes for their choir members — in the Latin context this is luxurious. If instead, more of the middle-class churches themselves were to teach a Biblical perspective about stewardship, about the danger of accumulating material possessions, about the needs of the poor, Christ would be the answer to many more people.

Needed: More Mordecais

Many Gospel People shun politics. A few, however, believe that the basic system in a given country is so corrupt, so heavily weighted against most of the people, that any attempt at political reform is simply applying band-aids to a patient needing massive surgery. It should not surprise us, therefore, that Christians fought with the rebels in the Mexican revolution, or were in large force among the Sandinistas who overthrew the Somozas in Nicaragua, or participated in revolutions in the Dominican Republic, Chile, or Guatemala.

In the 1980s, when almost all of the many heavy-handed military governments gave way to more democratic regimes, the growing number of evangelicals was acquiring more voting power. The possibilities of evangelicals getting elected became real. The current president of Guatemala is an *evangélico* and evangelicals are ranking government leaders in several countries — Peru and Brazil to mention two.

The newly elected evangelical is often naive and lacks experience. Just because he is "born again" does not necessarily make him a good president, mayor, congressman or local school board member. One evangelical with political savvy in Brazil's capital considers himself a "Mordecai", giving orientation to the "Esthers" who have been elected to legislature.

Evangelical political parties? Only a few years ago such an idea would have been absurd. Colombia, the most Catholic of countries, awoke with surprise in 1990 to learn that an evangelically-oriented party won two seats in an assembly charged with rewriting the constitution. Politics can be as treacherous as a mine field for the Gospel People. But for better or worse, there are evangelically-oriented parties in Venezuela and Costa Rica.

Political issues differ from those in the U.S. Abortion is hardly an issue — most Latin Americans are shocked to learn that it is legal in the U.S. Prayer in public schools? Latin evangelicals are usually on the side of removing religion from the public schools. Schoolroom religion has been traditionally strictly Roman Catholic.

But the live issue may be the school board that delays payments of teachers' salaries in order to gain profit on interest. Meanwhile the teachers and their families suffer greatly. The evangelical middle-of-the-road Latin American Theological Fraternity is on the cutting-edge of motivating and providing theological bases for participation by Christian leaders in the political and societal arena through its conferences, seminars, and writings. In its 1983 conference in the Dominican Republic on "Christians and Political Action", for example, participants looked at issues of justice, peace and democracy in the Latin society from the standpoint of the Kingdom of God. In October of 1991 a conference in Buenos Aires focused on the role of evangelical political parties.

All of the Above

How can Christ be the answer in Latin America? Seeing people "born again" through evangelism? Churches ministering compassionately to the world about them? Christians penetrating society as salt and light? Political action? It takes all of the above.

The Chilean Pentecostal may be told by his pastor to stay out of sinful politics. But as he helps his Christian brother to pay his light bill this month he provides a micro-solution to a desperate micro-situation. The Christian professor teaching sociology at the university, on the other hand, will think in terms of macro-solutions. Both are necessary.

Of course, the real macro-solution is Christ's return to establish the visible kingdom. A perfect society on earth is not now possible nor expected. The hope of the Lord's coming spurs the Gospel People on to show forth signs of the coming kingdom in bearing witness to Jesus Christ by word, deed, and example.

"We want jobs!" This was the appeal Tony Campolo shouted during his address at an InterVarsity Urbana missions conference. Campolo, sociology professor and evangelist, was echoing the cry of the Third World poor looking for employment — not handouts or recreational facilities. At Eastern College in Pennsylvania Campolo founded a program offering an MBA designed to equip Christians to go or return to Third World countries and set up small businesses which will provide these jobs.

Christians in the U.S. can encourage and help Latin American brothers and sisters in carrying out their Kingdom work in many ways. Here are some:
- We can vote for presidents and congressmen and women who are concerned about human rights in Latin America and elsewhere.
- We can become involved in international efforts in Latin America providing relief in times of emergency and crisis, funding community development projects among the urban poor and the hordes of street children in all of the cities, and by planting trees through our gifts.
- Our churches can link up with Latin American churches working through mission organizations.
- We can participate in short-term service trips to a Latin American country or help support such programs.
- We can befriend and relate to Hispanic believers in the U.S. who are in need and who have needy families back home.
- Given the flow of many Hispanics to and from North America, every Hispanic won to Christ in the U.S. may be a missionary to family and friends abroad.

Above all, our prayers can make the difference. Prayer sustains the Gospel People as they lead their neighbors to Christ, comfort the grieving, bless the needy, and work toward changing their society.

SUGGESTED FURTHER READING:

-   Howard Snyder *A Kingdom Manifesto* (InterVarsity Press of Downer's Grove, IL, 1985). An exposition by a former missionary to Brazil calling for the church to be genuinely holistic in its ministry as it gets on with its kingdom work.

-   Paul Borthwick *How to Be a World Class Citizen* (Victor Books of Wheaton, IL, 1991). A practical, readable book about how to become involved in mission locally and in other parts of the world, including Latin America.

CHAPTER SEVENTEEN

A Christ for Latin America

"The man had ninety-nine old women in his corral, but he realized that one was missing. So, he went into the desert to find her," said the new missionary. He labored through the story with his limited Spanish.

One mistake, confusing *vieja* ("old lady") with *oveja* ("sheep"), made that yet one more story to add to the repertoire of true accounts and legends of how missionaries fail — either by a mistake in language or failing to adapt to the local culture.

The mistakes of many new missionaries can be tolerated (and Latin Americans are usually very tolerant), but there are broader, more sweeping issues to be considered. What kind of picture de we paint as we describe the Lord and His ministry? How wide and far-reaching is God's plan as we describe it?

Which Christ?

We mentioned earlier that according to John Mackay, the "other Spanish Christ" was left behind when the *conquistadores* came to America. The true Christ did not arrive. The Christ of the *conquistadores* was a misrepresentation, an imposter who appeared in Spanish or Portuguese wrappings. What were these visible vestments? Lust for gold, exploitation of human labor, cruel racial bigotry, and a legalistic, guilt-ridden, superstitious dead religion. The "Other Spanish Christ" was the more spiritual, the Christ of the mystics and reformers.

Nearly four hundred years later, Protestant missionaries appeared on the scene. What kind of Christ did they bring?

—Was He nothing more than the Christ of the U.S. Bible-belt revivals, with an exclusive accent on personal repentance and regeneration?

—Did they leave behind the other Christ of the Protestant tradition?

—The Christ of Lord Shaftesbury, the evangelical statesman who spearheaded the British reform movement in the 19th century?

—The Christ of William Wilberforce who as a Christian helped abolish slavery in Great Britain?

—The Christ of those Christians who fought against slavery in the U.S.?

—The Christ of William Booth of the Salvation Army?

—The Christ of the Wesleys who linked evangelistic fervor with social concern?

—The Christ of George Whitefield who ministered to the poor masses?

In many cases the Christ with a heart to meet all human need was left behind. Missionaries to Latin America have not always presented this compassionate Christ.

On the other hand, we may be wrong in regretting that neither *conquistadores* nor Protestant missionaries brought to Latin America the fullest and truest expressions of the gospel. In fact, the Gospel People should be looking neither to the Other Spanish Christ nor to the Other Protestant Christ. Rather they should find the Christ of the Scriptures who reveals Himself in a way that specifically meets their needs today.

He is the Christ Who reveals Himself in power to answer the prayer of the needy, the sick, and the demon possessed.

He is the Christ Who reveals Himself in the Scriptures and illumines our pathway through visions, dreams, or spiritual intuition.

He is the Christ Who fills a heart with true *fiesta*.

He is the Christ Who mingles with the poor as well as with the jet-setters.

He is the Christ Who softens our heart towards the needy.

He is the Christ Who shares our hungering and thirst for righteousness and justice when society's cards are stacked against the hopeless.

He is the Christ Who empowers ordinary people to tell their neighbors about the gospel.

He is the Christ Who can reinforce the integrity of the Latin

Christian politician and businessman.

He is the Christ, too, Who answers the questions of the Latin American intellectuals.

He is the Christ Who is real to people in their culture — right where they are — and is true to what the Scriptures tell us about Him.

The Christ of Two Realities

The largest evangelical church in Caracas, Venezuela, is *La Iglesia Evangélica Pentecostal Las Acacias*. It began by reaching out to the city's people — by offering telephone counseling. The response was overwhelming. The people reached by phone formed a congregation that eventually bought a huge old cinema seating 2000 and occupying an entire city block.

The Spirit-filled evangelistic witness of the church is clear and uncompromising. The church is helping meet the needs of the surrounding depressed neighborhoods with medical and legal services, marriage and family counseling. Most recently, they helped establish a drug rehabilitation center, the *Hogar Nueva Vida* ("New Life Home").

The Las Acacias Church lives and serves in the light of two great realities — the spiritual and the physical. The Christ of this church is Lord of both the spiritual "heavenlies" as well as the nitty-gritty pain-filled and hungry "real" world.

To Move a Mountain, Start with Prayer

The spiritual world is not that far removed from the physical. We see this also in the way spiritual activity — prayer — impacts the world we see around us.

Following the 1989 murder of Colombian presidential hopeful Luis Galán and at a time of tremendous pressure by guerrillas and the drug cartels, more than 80 of 100 Medellín congregations held simultaneous all-night prayer vigils.

The Gospel People unconsciously make connections between the spiritual and natural. For them, the spiritual battle is literal and real — as seen in a child-like faith in God in every aspect of life, in dreams and visions, in praying for healing, in all-night prayer vigils, and in recognition of the presence of demons and the practice of exorcism.

There is a great dependence on the power of the Spirit of God against the onslaughts of Satan upon their individual and corporate lives.

Dealing with Visible Realities

Intimately related to the spiritual struggles with Satanic principalities and powers is the concern of the "Las Acacias Church" and other such congregations across Latin America with the other side of the coin — the physical realities of this world and particularly the condition of the poor and the outcasts.

The *Iglesia Evangélica Bautista La Lucila* in Buenos Aires, Argentina, is a middle-class church with a concern for the poor and, more recently, for the drug addicts in that great city.

Some years ago the church opened its doors to a "virtual invasion" of young drug addicts. Some even came to church "high."

With time, and through heavy doses of Christian love, most of these young people stayed. Many came to know Christ and today are leaders in the church.

But many barriers had to be overcome before this could happen. In 1972, a former addict came to Christ and began to reach out to his friends, nearly all of them drug dependent.

When he requested permission to bring them to church, it was granted. But when a score of them started showing up, people became uneasy.

Things came to a head when a church officer suggested that special activities be programmed for the drug addicts, excluding them from the main worship services. In response, a pastor pointed out that this congregation could either become "a closed synagogue of Pharisees" or an "open church." "Which will we be?" he asked.

Perhaps reluctantly they concluded that the church is for sinners. The succeeding months were not easy. But the believers "hung in there." The Lord not only blessed the church and many addicts accepted Christ, but a far-reaching drug outreach and rehabilitation program, broader than the La Lucila Church, was born.

Not all Latin American evangelical churches share this vision. It often takes a second generation of believers to awaken to the need to address this second reality. North American Christians of the Post-Cold War era may easily forget this reality when they think of Latin America. Just because Marxism fell in Eastern Europe does not mean that poverty and the causes for revolution in Latin America have evaporated. Massive poverty still exists.

The Gospel People are still in great danger in some countries where the Cold War became hot and never really cooled off. Early in 1991 Shining Path terrorists attacked the village of Ceano in Peru's south-central Andes. Two terrorists burst into a Pentecostal church prayer vigil and opened fire — killing 32 (including six children) and wounding 11. Some miraculously escaped through a window. The terrorists were apparently retaliating against Ceano for villagers' participation in civil-defense patrols.

On a mountainside overlooking Mexico City, 160 *evangélicos* gathered in 1990 for an all-night prayer vigil in behalf of the capital. Although the site was far from any home, in the nearest villages church bells rang out to assemble a mob to drive out the Protestant "invaders." With stones, guns and dogs, a mob of fanatics forced the evangelicals to flee. Only through God's protection and the intervention of ten patrol cars of police did the believers escape death.

In contexts of drugs, poverty, and violence, the Gospel People can provide much more than a mere distraction from the realities of life. To overwhelming problems they are beginning to provide lasting solutions to people's problems. Redemptive hope, the restoration of broken lives and families, a fresh incentive to live and work, and an open door to a community of sisters and brothers are all signs of the Kingdom of God among the Gospel People.

One Christ, Lord of One Church

Along with the reality of the One Christ in the spiritual and the physical, there is a need in the Latin American evangelical church for unity. The Gospel People have not always displayed this oneness as members of the one Body of Christ. But there are beginnings of a new spirit of mutual respect and acceptance of one another.

Until recently there were two ministerial associations among evangelicals in Barranquilla, Colombia. To make matters worse, the two groups had a long history of feuding.

All of that changed when both groups attended a pastors retreat sponsored by LAM's Christ for the City (CFC) ministry. The theme of the gathering was the unity of the Body.

During the retreat a leader of one group felt convicted and suddenly proposed that his group be dissolved, adding that he was convinced that the city's pastors should form one association. God must have been at work because then and there everyone agreed.

Little wonder that in the months following, Barranquilla's evangelical churches grew 35% with 6000 new Christians through cooperative CFC evangelistic efforts.

The linkage between unity of the Body and evangelistic impact is a strong one. "I pray also for those who will believe in me through their message, that all of them may be one, Father, just as you are in me and I am in you. May they also be in us so that the world may believe that you have sent me.... May they be brought to complete unity to let the world know that you sent me and have loved them even as you have loved me" (Gospel of John, chapter 17).

Needed: a Christ for Latin America

Unity must cross international borders too. The Gospel People and Christians everywhere need to become increasingly sensitive to the common bond we enjoy in Christ and with one another throughout the world. As never before, Christians on this globe have greater access to communication with one another.

We can help each other. We can pray for one another. We can bear

one another's burdens. We can enrich each other's knowledge and faith by reflecting Christ in the diversity of our backgrounds and cultures. We can share our vision and our hope. Theologians from north and south, east and west can exchange insights the Holy Spirit gives them in their respective cultures and arrive at new and fresh implications from the Scriptures. We can become one in Christ — praying together and sharing the good news with others.

Millions are joining the ranks of the Gospel People. This means the majority are first generation Christians, with the traditional new believers' "first love" and enthusiasm. Really, the proportion of the population represented by the Gospel People does not matter as much as the vitality of that proportion. And this vitality is beginning to transform the Latin American scene.

Come with us to a retreat where Juan Isáis, veteran Mexican evangelist, is encouraging Latin American Christians to witness to their neighbors. There is prayer. There is exhortation from the Word. Above all there is singing. A favorite is *Mensajero del Gran Rey, Yo Soy, Yo Soy* ("I am a Messenger of the Great King"). They sing the chorus over and over. Their enthusiasm is infectious, the discouraged get encouraged, the unmotivated get motivated. Tomorrow they will be telling people about Christ, and soon there will be more believers in Him — more Gospel People.

The numbers grow, the churches too. Because they are convinced that they are Messengers of the King.

SUGGESTED FURTHER READING:

- John Maust *Peace and Hope in the Corner of the Dead* (Latin America Mission of Miami, 1987). In graphic narrative style with on-the-scene full-color photos this book relates the ongoing violence against *evangélicos* in Peru.

- Eugene Nida *Understanding Latin Americans* (William B. Carey Library of Pasadena, 1974). A readable, solid presentation of the points of cultural differences between Latin Americans and North Americans.

- William Dyrness *Learning About Theology from the Third World* (Zondervan Publishing House of Grand Rapids, 1991). This work emphasizes the vital importance of doing theology cross-culturally with Asian, African, Latin American, European and North American participation.

Epilogue
(Continued from the Prologue)

After a year in Bible school, Ana María married Ernesto and soon they had two children. As a guard at the entrance of an office building, Ernesto filled in his empty hours studying to complete a high school diploma in an extension program. And many more hours digging into the Scriptures.

Together they helped start a small neighborhood house-church. But Ana María's dreams really came true when they were invited by a *Christ for the City* team to join them in founding a new church on the other side of town.

Acres of squatters' shacks had appeared there almost overnight. The government stepped in, laying out streets and building concrete shells of houses which the occupants themselves could finish while acquiring them on easy payments.

The homes, all attached to each other in neat rows, represent an improvement, but the neighborhood is still more needy, more crime-ridden and more violent than the *barrio* where Ana María spent her childhood.

The team's nurse gives classes in first-aid and there is a program to tutor children after school. Ernesto and a team-mate have started dozens of home Bible studies. Soon the people transformed by Christ will become one more witnessing church.

In the most squalid *barrios* of tropical Latin America God provides splashes of beauty and color — the flowers growing out of the used paint cans on the porches, or simply growing wild along the fences. Antonio, Ana María, Ernesto and millions of other Gospel People are also God's splashes of color and hope to a drab and needy continent.

Index of major topics

About the authors

Clayton L. ("Mike") Berg, Jr. and *Paul E. Pretiz* have been missionaries with the Latin America Mission since 1956 and 1953, respectively. Pretiz is a communications specialist and musician with broad service in radio, evangelism, and Mission administration in many parts of Latin America and presently resides in Costa Rica. Berg lives in Miami and is a former president of the LAM, having also previously served as president of the Spanish language publishing house, Editorial Caribe, and as a professor of Christian education in Costa Rica. Both men were involved in the founding and early development of LAM's "Christ for the City" movement.